Kitchen Arabic

Kitchen Arabic

How My Family Came to America
and the Recipes We Brought with Us

JOSEPH GEHA

The University of Georgia Press ➤➤➤ Athens

Published by the University of Georgia Press
Athens, Georgia 30602
www.ugapress.org
© 2023 by Joseph Geha
All rights reserved
Designed by Erin Kirk
Set in Minion
Printed and bound by Integrated Books International
The paper in this book meets the guidelines for
permanence and durability of the Committee on
Production Guidelines for Book Longevity of the
Council on Library Resources.

Most University of Georgia Press titles are available
from popular e-book vendors.

Printed in the United States of America
27 26 25 24 23 P 5 4 3 2 1

Library of Congress Control Number: 2022947098
ISBN: 9780820364001 (paperback)
ISBN: 9780820364018 (epub)
ISBN: 9780820364025 (PDF)

For my grandchildren . . .

Ruthie,
Wilson,
and Joey

. . . with love

➤➤➤

Contents

Kitchen Arabic

Prologue

In September 1946, on the evening before my family was to set off on our journey of emigration to America, my five-year-old sister, VeeVee, began running a high fever. Our parents didn't dare call a doctor. Typhoid had been rampant throughout Lebanon all that summer and early fall; just the suspicion of it would be enough to prevent us from boarding the ship. And because my father had already paid bribes to cover not only what transit documents we lacked but also the further payoffs needed to secure us a berth on the *Vulcania*, the first passenger ship leaving Beirut harbor after the war, we simply couldn't afford to postpone our departure. We would have to board tomorrow, or never.

To quiet VeeVee's moans, my mother gave her laudanum, a tincture of opium. It wasn't hard to come by, every *pharmacieh* in Beirut sold it over the counter. Mama gave it to us children whenever she felt we were agitated or cranky. It quieted us and helped us to sleep.

Mama made *rishta* soup for supper, and later that night, while my sister and brother and I dreamed our opium dreams, our father hatched a plan that was to become a family story.

→ → →

In Syrian tradition, storytellers begin with the phrase *kaan makaan*, a kind of Arabic "once upon a time." Translated literally, *kaan makaan* means "it happened, it didn't happen." In other words, *Here's a story; maybe it happened* (kaan)*; then again maybe it didn't* (makaan) . . . *You decide.*

So, here's the story as I heard it all my growing up. Early next morning, Baba (Arabic, which has no *p* sound, substitutes a *b*) roused VeeVee and had Mama rouge her fever-yellowed cheeks, dress her in a bright frock, and tie a large, jaunty bow in her hair.

Later, waiting in line at the docks, Baba held VeeVee, weak and listless, in his arms. Then, as our turn came to ascend the gangplank, he began to tickle her. And that was how, giggling and annoyed but at least animated, she made it past the ship's medical officer, who stood watching as the passengers were checked in. Baba waited until after we'd settled into our steerage quarters. In an hour we could feel the ship moving. In another hour or so, we were out of sight of land, and Baba carried VeeVee to the top deck. "You! Come here!" he called out to the first crew member he came across. "Your ship has bad water! See how sick it made her!"

The crew member took one look, and my sister was immediately carried to the ship's hospital. There she spent the entire fifteen-day voyage.

She remembers a nurse reading to her and another nurse painting her fingernails. My brother, Aboody, a year older than I, remembers Baba holding him up so that he could see the dolphins leaping in our wake. As for me, not quite two, I remember nothing. Not the ship, not the seasickness I was told we suffered, not the shouting that went up from all the decks as we steamed past the Statue of Liberty. For me it would be only a story, one of so many I heard, *kaan makaan*, all my growing up. My sister had recovered by the time we reached New York, but our arrival story doesn't end there.

Authorities in the medical facility at Ellis Island had been notified of VeeVee's condition and, after examining her, decided that she must remain in quarantine for another two full weeks. So too must the rest of the family. And quarantined along with us for every single day of those two weeks was every single other—very disgruntled, I imagine—passenger, officer, and crew member of the *Vulcania*.

We were released from Ellis Island on Saturday, October 5, 1946. I know the date because, as my family told the story, it took forever to find a taxi that day in Manhattan, that day being Yom Kippur, and the majority of New York cabbies in those days being Jewish. That's how we arrived and how it happened that we can add our names to the multitudes who underwent processing at Ellis Island. *Kaan makaan.*

→ → →

Rishta, our last meal in the old country, is served traditionally to observe fresh starts, like the setting off on a journey or the occasion of a child's first tooth.

The recipe itself can be as complex or simple as you'd like—the essential ingredients are lentils, coriander, onions, and greens. For a vegetarian (or Lenten) version, use water instead of chicken stock.

Rishta
(Lentil Soup)

10 cups chicken stock
1 cup brown lentils
2 tablespoons butter
¼ cup olive oil
1 medium onion, chopped
Salt
4 large garlic cloves, pounded to a paste with a little coarse salt
½ teaspoon black pepper
2 tablespoons dried crushed mint
1 tablespoon ground coriander
1 tablespoon ground cumin
1 cup chopped fresh cilantro
½ cup chopped scallions
4 ounces noodles (see notes below)
10 ounces chopped spinach
¼ cup fresh-squeezed lemon juice
2 lemons, each cut into 4 wedges

1. Pour the stock into a 4-quart saucepan, add the lentils, and bring to a boil. Reduce heat, cover, and simmer 20 minutes.
2. Meanwhile, heat the butter and olive oil in a 10- to 12-inch fry pan. Add the onion (with a light sprinkle of salt to release its water) and sauté until slightly browned.
3. Add the garlic, pepper, mint, coriander, and cumin to the onions; fry for a minute more; add the cilantro and scallions, stirring 2 minutes, then carefully add the mixture to the lentils.
4. Add the noodles and 2 teaspoons salt, or to taste; continue to simmer 15 minutes.
5. Add the spinach and simmer another 5 minutes. Stir in the lemon juice. Serve with wedges of lemon.

Serves 8

NOTES:

- Use store-bought egg noodles, broken up spaghetti, or make your own noodles by mixing together . . .

  ½ cup all-purpose flour
  1 tablespoon olive oil
  1 pinch salt
  2 tablespoons water

  . . . to form a dough. Let dough rest 10 to 15 minutes, then roll out on flour-dusted surface into a squarish shape, and cut into ¼-inch by 3-inch strips and add directly to the *rishta*. Give a gentle stir to keep them from sticking together.

  To deepen the flavor, the noodles (whether store-bought or homemade) can be roasted on a cookie sheet in the oven at 350°F for about 15 to 20 minutes (or until golden brown) before adding to soup.

- One cup of coarsely chopped Swiss chard can be added with the spinach, and for a more robust meal, a cup or so of rinsed canned kidney beans.

- Serving *rishta*, it's nice to place a bowl of roasted chickpeas on the table for passing around with the lemon wedges. To roast chickpeas, drain and rinse canned chickpeas, pat dry with paper towels, and toss in olive oil and 1 teaspoon salt. Roast in 400°F oven for 20 to 30 minutes. While still hot, toss with 1 teaspoon ground cumin and 1 pinch or 2 of cayenne pepper.

One

Kitchen Arabic

Immigrant children first speak the language of their mothers, and for me, that language was Arabic. My mother's soft Damascene dialect explained my world to me, taught me my first life lessons, entertained me with stories. It gave me names for the foods that nourished me. It was in Arabic that my childish fears were eased and I was comforted to sleep at bedtime. It was the language of my first prayers and my most personal thoughts. Even today, in my seventies, all I need do is whisper to myself "Zuzu," the Arabic diminutive of my childhood name, and that's enough to make the past come alive again.

My father had been to America before, back at the turn of the twentieth century, when he was a twelve-year-old stowaway; so, on this, his second emigration, he was prepared to shepherd us from station to station in a broken but passable English. After we'd debarked the ferry to Manhattan, a taxi took us to the Middle Eastern enclave along Atlantic Avenue in Brooklyn, where we stayed two weeks while Baba arranged for train tickets to Toledo, Ohio, the city where he'd spent his first sojourn in America.

Now, in 1946, New York's Grand Central Terminal observed an elegant, longstanding tradition: every day at 6:00 p.m., a plush crimson carpet specially designed for the Twentieth Century Limited was unrolled so that passengers could walk on it as they boarded. Borrowed from the protocols of European nobility, this practice proved so popular that it entered the American lexicon. Years afterward we could recount in a family story how, upon our arrival, America had given us "the red-carpet treatment." *Literally.*

➤ ➤ ➤

In Toledo, Baba opened a small grocery-butcher shop on Monroe Street, not far from the North End neighborhood nicknamed Little Syria, and we lived in an apartment upstairs from the store. It was a small flat with two bedrooms and a potbellied coal stove in the front room; in the kitchen, next to the wooden icebox, stood a laundry tub with a hand-cranked wringer attached. The icebox had an upper compartment that needed to be replenished regularly with ice and a galvanized tray below to catch the meltwater. Every couple of days or so I used to watch in awe as the ice man stamped up our stairs hefting on his shoulder a huge block of ice, gripped by tongs. His shoulder was sheathed in leather, and the block of ice flecked with sawdust. Another early memory is of listening as my parents called to one another up and down that same staircase—Mama, one hand on the banister, asking something about tonight's meal, and at the bottom Baba in his white apron, one foot propping open the store's screen door, repeating for her the step-by-step procedure on how to prepare kibbeh or *koosa* or whatever it was we were having for supper.

Mama needed the help, because when my parents were first married, she didn't know a thing about cooking. Which was ironic since she'd grown up in a household of cooks—her mother, grandmother, two aunts, seven sisters. But she was one of the youngest in that family and so found herself more often than not being shooed out of the kitchen. Baba on the other hand, a through-and-through Lebanese male, prided himself on his culinary ability, which he saw as essentially a masculine art. How even more ironic it was, then, that Mama quickly surpassed him; more than a fast learner, she proved to be a natural in the kitchen.

Adopting a new language, however, was another story. My mother was reluctant to abandon Arabic. Something of an introvert, she felt self-conscious attempting to speak English even at home. She viewed the "Amerkain" as a fast-talking, impatient lot, especially those who tried to coax her along by raising the volume of their voices, finishing her sentences, suggesting words to fill her hesitant pauses. "Listen to the radio!" I remember my father urging her, and the rest of us as well, believing that English would sink in, as if by osmosis. Simple as it may sound, he had a point. Language is a living thing and as such it changes with use, adapting itself to new situations and necessities. And like it or not, changing language changes the user as well. Immersed in the back-ground noise of radio and movies and eventually television, even to the repetitive lessons her children brought home from school—Mama, like all of us, made the transition. Even so, her English would always be broken, sprinkled with malapropisms, and so heavily accented that it often sounded very much like, well, Arabic.

Oddly enough, at the same time, her Arabic was beginning to sound a lot like English. As was our whole family's Arabic. And it wasn't just us. The same thing had happened, and would continue to happen, all over Little Syria. The cause was human nature, the result of an accumulation of little changes arising out of convenience. The process went something like this: you're on the phone, say, chattering away in Arabic, and as sometimes happens in conversation, you hit a mental blip ("What's the word for . . . ?"). But instead of breaking rhythm and losing your train of thought, you automatically go with the first word that fits the bill. So what if it's the English word for what you mean? You simply tack an Arabic ending onto it and keep going, finish your thought. Do that enough times, and even though you sound old-country, even though your words have Arabic endings and your sentences Arabic-like syntax arrangements, you're not really speaking Arabic anymore but a hybrid patois that in Little Syrias all over America would come to be called Kitchen Arabic.

Here's an example: the simple declarative sentence *Souq il sierrah al mahal* (Drive the car to the store) is transmogrified via Kitchen Arabic into *Darrif il cahr al stahrr*. The words *sound* Arabic, all right, but newcomers from the old country can barely make them out (once they stop rolling their eyes in puzzlement), and Americans, if they listen carefully enough, almost can make them out!

So why do we call this mishmash *Kitchen* Arabic?

Because children first speak the language of their mothers, and in Little Syria, if you wanted to find your mother, the first place you'd go to look for her would be the *matbakh*, or kitchen. Many of today's immigrants can use Skype right there on their smart phones to keep in touch with folks back in the old country, but in those "radio days" of old before the luxuries of hot running water or freezers, ample refrigeration, or blenders or microwaves, the kitchen was where an immigrant mother usually had to be, snapping peas or rolling grape leaves while she waited for the dough to rise. The kitchen was where she did laundry, too, where she mended and ironed and hung clothes to dry in the winter. We ate our meals at the kitchen table. That chipped, enamel-topped table was also the closest thing we had to a desk, and so it was in the kitchen that we could find Mama writing letters home to the old country (unlike Baba, she was literate, having had three years' schooling), and where I remember her sitting to memorize the Pledge of Allegiance for her citizenship exam. At night, having put us children to bed, it was at the kitchen table where she sat praying her rosary, waiting for Baba to close the store and come upstairs for his evening meal, kept warm by the huge cast-iron stove's robust pilot light.

In that kitchen, my mother took special pride in the Arabic dishes she cooked, cherishing that aspect of her heritage, which unlike language, changed very little over time and distance, and which spoke to her then, an exile on this new continent, as it speaks to me now, of joy and comfort and love.

➜ ➜ ➜

Kibbeh, spiced lamb ground up with onions and bulghur wheat, was a favorite of my father's, and it was one of the first dishes Mama learned to make for him.

Considered the national dish of Lebanon, kibbeh was originally made by placing the ingredients in the hollow of a large stone and pounding them into a pasty mixture. In America, Mom's generation used meat grinders made of heavy cast metal that you clamped to the kitchen counter and cranked by hand. These days, we've graduated to food processors.

Kibbeh can be served raw like a steak tartare (*kibbeh nayeh*) or formed into hollow little football shapes, stuffed with pine nuts and onion, and deep fried (*kibbeh raas*). The name itself derives from the Arabic word for "ball." But since kibbeh is an important ingredient in many other dishes, its most versatile form would be baked in a pan (*kibbeh b'il saniyeh*), which also happens to be the version said to be preferred by the cooks of my hometown, Zahlé, near the northern rim of the Beqaa Valley.

Kibbeh b'il Saniyeh
(Ground Lamb with Bulghur and Onion Bake)

THE FILLING:
3 tablespoons butter
¼ cup pine nuts
3/4 pound ground lamb
1 teaspoon crushed dried mint leaves (optional)
1 medium onion, chopped fine
1 teaspoon ground nutmeg
2 teaspoons ground cinnamon

1 teaspoon allspice
½ teaspoon salt
1 teaspoon black pepper

1. Melt butter in a fry pan; add pine nuts and sauté until starting to color.
2. Add the meat, breaking it up as you sauté, 10 minutes.
3. Add the remaining ingredients and sauté till the onion is translucent; set aside.

THE KIBBEH:

1 cup #1 bulghur (see note, below)
1½ tablespoons Lebanese seven-spice mix (see recipe for
    Baharat on page 152)
1¼ pounds ground lamb
1 medium onion, roughly chopped
1½ teaspoons ground cinnamon
1 teaspoon allspice
1 teaspoon salt
1 teaspoon black pepper
Pinch of cayenne pepper (optional)
Ice water
¼ cup olive oil
3 tablespoons butter (cut into about 12 to 15 pieces) (optional)
Sprigs of parsley for garnish

1. Place bulghur in a small bowl and fill to overrunning with a slow stream of cold tap water, continuing until any floating chaff runs off. Cover the bulghur in tap water and let soak 15 to 20 minutes, then drain in a strainer, squeezing out excess water with hands.
2. Add the bulghur and seven-spice mix to bowl of food processor and run on high for about 6 to 8 seconds. Remove and knead, adding a dribble or two of water as needed to achieve a wet-sand/clay consistency.
3. Butter the sides and bottom of a 9-by-12-inch baking dish.
4. In a large bowl, mix together ground meat, onion, and spices to a pasty consistency, wetting hands in ice water as needed.
5. Add this mixture in batches to the bowl of a food processor and pulse (adding ice water or chips of ice as needed) until all is well ground and mixed.
6. Knead the meat and bulghur mixtures together until well mixed.
7. Divide the raw kibbeh in half; with one half, break off small sections and roll into ping-pong-ball-sized pieces, and pat them flat to a thickness of about ½ inch on the bottom of a well-greased baking pan until you've

created a layer that goes up the sides a bit. Moistening hands with cold water, smooth and even out the layer.

8. Sprinkle evenly with the stuffing; then top the stuffing with the remaining half of the kibbeh, pressing it down nice and firm; moistening hands with ice water, smooth the top.

9. Deeply score a diamond-shaped pattern into the top. Press a hole in center with your finger, then run a knife around the edges of the pan. Drizzle lightly with olive oil, then, if you like, dot the top with butter.

(We now let the kibbeh rest 1 hour before continuing. I don't know why, Mom said we just do. Can't hurt.)

10. Bake 45 minutes at 400°F on lower rack; raise to middle rack and broil 5 minutes or till browned on top.

11. Garnish diamond-sized portions with parsley. Serve hot with cold Laban Sauce and a shot of arak.

Tip: Not too lean on the lamb! Lamb shoulder is best; if using beef, choose top round, 80 percent lean to 20 percent fat.

Note: Bulghur (or bulgur) is wheat grain that has been parboiled, dried, and ground, and it's often mistakenly called cracked wheat, which is not parboiled. An essential ingredient in tabouli and kibbeh, bulghur comes in four grinds, fine #1, medium #2, coarse #3, and extra coarse #4. It can be found not only in Middle Eastern specialty stores but also in large supermarkets and health-food stores, as well as online. Same goes for tahini, or sesame seed butter, which most readers will recognize as a major ingredient in hummus dip.

Serves 8

➤ ➤ ➤

Laban is essential to Lebanese cuisine. Essentially fermented cow's milk (or goat's if you can get it), *laban* is what gave Lebanon its nickname, the Land of Milk and Honey. Here's a *laban* recipe for one of our basic sauces.

Laban Tahini Sauce

¼ cup water
1½ tablespoons tahini paste
8 ounces plain yogurt
1 tablespoon lemon juice
1 garlic clove, crushed and minced, or ½ teaspoon garlic powder
1 tablespoon dried mint (or 2 tablespoons fresh, chopped fine)
1 teaspoon salt, or to taste
1 tablespoon olive oil

1. In a small bowl, whisk water, a spoonful at a time, into the tahini paste. Stir the mixture into the yogurt.
2. Add the lemon juice, garlic, mint, salt, and olive oil to the tahini-yogurt mixture. Whisk well and place in fridge to cool.

AUNT SOPHIE'S TAHINI TIPS:
1. In any tahini sauce, mix in the water before the lemon juice, as this always makes for a whiter-looking sauce. Add the water gradually. Tahini thickens at first, but as you continue to stir, it will soon thin to the mayonnaiselike consistency that you're looking for.
2. Fresh garlic is best if using the sauce the same day you make it. This recipe stores for a few days in the fridge, but remember, raw garlic can grow botulism when anaerobic (as in tahini and/or olive oil), and so out of an abundance of caution, I feel that garlic powder is preferable if storing sauce for the week.

Two

Escape

At the beginning of the last century, America experienced what has come to be recognized as one of the largest migrations of human beings ever recorded. Over twelve million immigrants were processed at Ellis Island alone between 1892, when it began operations, and 1924, when an act of Congress effectively shut the flood down to a trickle.

My father, Elias Geha, was swept into that flood at its height. He was almost fourteen years old in the fall of 1901, shortly after President McKinley was assassinated, when he made the journey, traveling alone nearly halfway around the world from Zahlé, Lebanon, to New York City. Or so he claimed. There is no record of him being processed at Ellis Island. No record of his arrival, nor even of his ever having boarded a ship. The reason there are no records is, of course, another family story.

I'd heard it all my life, but now, setting it down in black and white, it looks to me almost like something out of the Brothers Grimm, a fairy tale complete with a saintly mother who dies giving birth to our hero, a callous father, a cruel stepmother, and a quest that promises to take the child far from home across an ocean to the golden streets of a golden land and happiness ever after. In that golden land the story even features a fairy godmother of sorts, Baba's elder sister, Yemnah, who'd cared for him like the mother he never had, right up until—while he was still a young boy—she married and emigrated to the United States with her husband.

The story opens in Zahlé, in the back bedroom of a darkened, mud-brick hovel, with Baba as a thirteen year old tied to a bedpost. It's his stepmother's idea of punishment. His father is not home. My *jiddu* (grandfather, in Arabic) is a tanner, and so is gone for days at a time, buying hides or selling finished leather goods. But even when he's around the house he is passive, acquiescing to his new wife's ways of running things. Granted, Baba was a born rascal and hell-raiser, and I have to allow my grandparents something, I suppose. Even so, the discipline goes too far, and for far too long. On the second night of this abuse, being lashed to a bedpost without food or water, much less leave to use the *sishmeh*, Baba is thirsty and hungry, and he has soiled himself. But he is above all angry. The anger sustains him as he keeps steadily tugging at the knots, stretching them out.

It is past midnight when a final yank releases his wrists. Moving quietly in the dark, he finds the gold liras his father keeps in a pocket of his Sunday trousers; then—what the hell—he undresses and steals the trousers themselves ("I took the rope they tied me with and I used it for a belt!"). Sneaking into the *oudet il mouneh*, or larder, he fills a leather sack with what food he can find—cheese, dried sausages—whatever will travel and not quickly spoil. It's a day's journey to Beirut. He's heard stories about dock workers at the harbor there who, for only a few silver *qirsh*, would sneak you aboard ship with the cargo. Outside, he pauses for a bellyful of water at the pump, then cinches tight his rope belt and takes off for America.

➤➤➤

After having escaped my grandparents, my hungry, belt-tightening father would finish his growing up in America, where he would later boast that he'd turned himself into a "self-made" man. Indeed, in the coming years he would make many things of himself—grocer, barber, bootlegger, as well as a clever and inventive cook who sometimes ventured beyond the basics of traditional Lebanese cuisine to create new recipes. Like the following, one of my all-time favorite dishes that I grew up with. It's both heartening and hearty, as well as incredibly delicious, and I suppose a descriptive name for it might be *batata mihshee*, or as Mom—who would later perfect the dish—always called it, "stuffy potatoes."

Batata Mihshee
(Stuffy Potatoes)

THE STUFFING:
2 tablespoons olive oil
¼ pound pork sausage (or ½ cup chickpeas)
¾ pound ground beef or lamb (or ¾ cup walnut pieces, chopped)
½ medium onion, chopped fine
3 (or more) garlic cloves, minced
¼ cup pine nuts
½ cup chopped fresh cilantro (or parsley, or a combination), divided
1½ tablespoons dried mint
1 teaspoon allspice
2½ teaspoons ground cinnamon
½ teaspoon salt
½ teaspoon black pepper

Prepare the stuffing: In a large fry pan, warm the olive oil on medium heat, add the meat (or chickpeas and walnuts in vegetarian version) and brown nicely (about 8 to 10 minutes). Stir in onion and garlic and cook about another 3 to 4 minutes. Add pine nuts and stir 1 minute or 2. Stir in ¼ cup of the cilantro, as well as the mint, allspice, cinnamon, salt, and pepper, and cook about 5 minutes more. Remove from heat, allow to cool.

THE TOPPING SAUCE:
1 tablespoon olive oil
2 tablespoons tomato paste
1 can (14.5 ounces) tomato sauce
1 can (28 ounces) crushed tomatoes
½ teaspoon allspice
1½ teaspoons ground cinnamon
¼ teaspoon salt
¼ teaspoon black pepper
½ teaspoon sugar
1 dollop (½ to 1 teaspoon) chocolate syrup (optional)

Prepare the topping sauce: Place oil in a saucepan, set heat to medium, and add the tomato paste, stirring till it begins to darken, about 2 to 3 minutes. Add cans of tomato sauce and tomatoes and bring to a boil; then reduce heat to low and let simmer 15 minutes. Stir in spices, then sugar, and for a different kick, a dollop of chocolate syrup.

THE POTATOES:

12 small potatoes (Yukon Golds or Michigans will work well), peeled, or 6 large potatoes, halved and peeled

Prepare the potatoes: Gently core potatoes using a zucchini corer—which is a real thing (see page 112)—or an apple corer, creating a hollow to about ¾ of the way into the potato. Set aside the corings.

Cook the cored potatoes (boil or steam for about 15 minutes) and let cool. Meanwhile, butter a 9-by-12-inch baking dish. When the potatoes are cool enough to handle, loosely fill each cavity with stuffing and place into baking dish, using the corings and leftover stuffing to prop and nestle them in, hole side up.

Pour topping sauce over all and bake at 350°F for 40 minutes. Sprinkle with remaining ¼ cup cilantro just before serving with rice.

Serves 8

And don't serve Batata Mihshee with just plain old rice but with Riz bi Siriyeh!

Riz bi Siriyeh
(Syrian Rice)

1½ cups rice
½ cup thin vermicelli, broken
½ cup pine nuts
4 tablespoons (½ stick) butter
1½ teaspoons salt
1½ cups broth (beef, chicken, or veggie)
2 cups water

Wash rice and drain. Sauté vermicelli and pine nuts in butter to brown (approximately 2 to 3 minutes). Add drained rice and salt and sauté another minute. Add broth and water. Let boil vigorously a minute or so. Reduce heat to low, cover, and cook about 15 minutes. Fluff with a fork and serve.

Serves 8

→ → →

Like Rishta, Ameh Maslouq is also a *snaniyeh* dish that's served on the occasion of a child's first tooth. The basic recipe dates back to the third century CE, commemorating Eid il Burbara (the Feast of Saint Barbara), who according to one version of her legend lived in ancient Baalbek, Lebanon (not far from my father's birthplace in Zahlé), and who, like him, also ran away from home. Escaping religious persecution from her own father who'd locked her up in a tower, she fled barefoot across a newly sown wheat field. As she ran, the wheat berries miraculously germinated and shot up to hide her.

Ameh Maslouq
(Boiled Wheat Berry Pudding)

8 cups water
1 cup wheat berries (unshelled), rinsed and drained
2 teaspoons anise seed (some prefer placing these in a tea infuser
    or in a cloth spice bag)
1½ teaspoons orange-blossom water
½ cup sugar
½ cup each of raisins, pine nuts, and/or pistachios for topping

1. Bring water and wheat to a boil. Cover, lower heat, and let cook gently.
2. After 20 minutes, add the anise seed.
3. When the wheat is tender (45 minutes to 1 hour), turn off heat, remove spice bag (if using), and stir in orange-blossom water and sugar.
4. Top with raisins and nuts and serve hot.

Serves 12

Three

Marseilles

Alone and a stowaway, not knowing how he would feed and shelter himself, uncertain even of his destination—that was how my father left the Old World. But it sure wasn't how he landed in the New. Oddly enough, about three weeks after being secreted aboard ship in Beirut harbor, thirteen-year-old Elias debarked in Manhattan as a first-class passenger traveling in the company of his "mother."

But how did that happen? Well, there was a story, of course, but the explanation it provided raised more questions than it answered. I had no problem with the first part, how he got himself stowed away. Back then, amid the crush of turn-of-the-century immigration traffic, Beirut was no different from Marseilles or New York or any other port city around the world; as Baba recounted it, the practice of accepting bribes to sneak stowaways aboard ships had become so routine as to be seen almost as a stevedore's perk.

Less clear to me was what happened to him in the early days of that three-week journey. According to the story, while the ship was docked overnight at Marseilles, he was discovered by a port inspector and promptly ejected from the ship. Worse, he soon realized that what little money he had left was missing. Stolen, no doubt, by a pickpocket working the crowded waterfront. So there he was, suddenly marooned in a foreign country, penniless and hungry and completely out of luck. Then, not five minutes later, his luck returned when a total stranger, a French doctor, approached him. He seemed to be a kindly fellow, offering to help out a panicked youth in trouble. This doctor could speak a little Arabic—how's that for a coincidence!—and he brought Baba to the harbor's large Arab district. There, in a hole-in-the-wall restaurant, he treated the youth to a bowl of *kishik* with kibbeh and cabbage. *Kibbit kishik*, so heartening and so familiar. Of course, the whole thing was too good to be true. Dad was young but could he have been *that* naive? Then again, I don't suppose you ask a lot of questions when you're hungry.

Leaving the restaurant, the doctor led young Elias up the street to a kind of tenement or rooming house, where the Arab landlord brought out scissors and trimmed Baba's hair. He was given a hot bath, then fitted with a complete change of clothes.

The shirt was worn and mended and a bit large for his small frame, but it was clean. And the trousers came with leather braces, so he wouldn't need that rope he'd been using for a belt. The jacket he was given was the same color and material as the trousers. A mirror stood in a corner of the room. Baba put on the jacket and buttoned it. He looked handsome in his new outfit. He had prominent cheekbones, dark eyes, and a wealth of curly hair, even after the trimming. Along his upper lip was the shadow of a mustache. Standing straight, he looked like a little man and was pleased. In those days, the idea wasn't for adults to try and look like teenagers, as it is today. Back then, young people were eager to leave childhood behind and dress like grown-ups, to adopt the mien and posture of adults.

Later that same evening, just before the ship was about to leave Marseilles harbor, the doctor brought my father back aboard, led him by hand up the gangplank, and deposited him in the elegant, first-class state room of a woman who was making the crossing alone. She wasn't young, but she wasn't old, either. And not bad looking. "Tall, with red hair," Baba would wag his head in fond remembrance. "An' onna way over, she taught me everything . . . ev-eree-a-ting!"

I was a kid when I first heard this story and so of course I had no idea what "everything" was. Not till I was well into adulthood did I begin to suspect what really had happened to my father, that he'd been caught up in the web of an elaborate racket. My suspicion was confirmed when, many years later, I was recounting Baba's story to a cousin who had recently immigrated from Lebanon. As he listened, the cousin began to nod his head yes, yes, the way you do when you know what's coming. "Then this doctor took care of him, right?" he interrupted. "Got him a bath, new clothes?" The cousin knew what was coming because he'd heard a similar story about a young male relative of his father's who'd come over alone just before the First World War, and this relative claimed that he wasn't the only one to whom something like that had happened while in Marseilles.

As for the doctor who rescued Baba, we concluded, he must have had an accomplice, or maybe even was himself the pickpocket. Either way, he was no doctor but some dockside pimp who serviced lonely travelers, part of a network that most likely stretched from the Marseilles port inspectors all the way back to the stevedores in Beirut harbor.

Today our modern sensibilities are outraged at the sexual exploitation of a child, but Baba never looked at it that way. He saw only the good in it for him: in his version of things, life had tossed him onto the ocean of the world, and to paraphrase Henry Miller, he'd floated like a cork.

So the reason why there's no record of my father being processed at Ellis Island in 1901 is because he never debarked there. In those days, before steamships docked at the island's Immigration Inspection Depot, they first stopped at one of the piers in lower Manhattan in order to let off their priority-class passengers. And it was there that my father walked down the gangplank, through the customs queue, and into America, holding the hand of his American, red-haired "mother."

➤➤➤

Kishik, like that my father was fed in Marseilles, is a mixture of wheat and *laban* that has been sun dried (traditionally on sheets spread out on the flat roofs of the village) then formed and further dried into hard, rocklike nuggets, or else pulverized into a powder. In either form it keeps forever and has been called the ultimate survival food. Lebanese immigrants who lived through the Great Depression in America made and stored away large amounts of *kishik*. Today, it can be found at Middle Eastern specialty stores or online at Amazon.

Kibbit kishik, a version that's one of my personal favorites, provides a taste of home that's especially heartening when December winds sweep across the dark prairies of the Midwest.

Here is my mother's version, therefore the cabbage, and the soupy rather than porridgelike texture. Leftovers will absorb liquid and need more broth when served again.

Kibbit Kishik
(Hearty Porridge)

¼ head of cabbage
8 (or more!) large garlic cloves
3 tablespoons butter
3 tablespoons olive oil
2 medium onions, sliced into crescents
1 cup *kishik* powder
1 teaspoon salt
Dash of cayenne or black pepper
3 cups chicken or vegetable broth (or more to adjust consistency)
4 (or more) baked kibbeh diamonds, crumbled (see Kibbeh b'il
    Saniyeh recipe on page 8)
1½ loaves pita, dried and/or toasted and broken into
    bite-size pieces

1. Steam the cabbage in an inch or so of water for 15 minutes in a covered pan. Remove the cabbage, let cool a bit, and slice into half-inch-wide strips. Set aside.
2. Crush and/or roughly slice the garlic. Set aside.
3. In a Dutch oven or a deep fry pan, bring the butter and olive oil to shimmering over medium-high heat.
4. Add onions and sauté until limp, 5 to 6 minutes, then add the garlic, lower the heat to medium, and sauté for another minute.
5. Sprinkle in the *kishik* powder while continuing to stir, as if making a roux.
6. Add salt and pepper.
7. After a couple minutes, when the *kishik* powder has begun to darken, carefully stir in the broth (using less for a porridgelike consistency, more for soupy), scraping up and deglazing the pan. Bring to a boil.
8. Reduce heat to a simmer, stir in the cabbage strips and the kibbeh.
9. Let simmer uncovered about 15 minutes.
10. Serve by ladling into soup bowls, each containing ¼ cup or so of toasted pita pieces.

Serves 4 to 6

➜ ➜ ➜

Necessity being the mother of invention, many of mankind's tastiest survival foods were developed out of the need to preserve perishables for travel or against hard times such as winter or drought. In the Old Country, foodstuffs preserved for later consumption are called *mouneh* and are stored in the *oudet il mouneh*, or *mouneh* room. Over the millennia, the processes of drying, pickling, salting, and smoking staple foods revealed new textures and flavor combinations. Here's a vegetarian dish that makes use of three of our most basic staples—onions, cabbage, and bulghur. It's called *marshoosheh*, and it's tasty served hot or cold.

Marshoosheh
(Cabbage Sauté)

2 tablespoons butter
¼ cup olive oil
1 large onion, sliced into crescents
1 teaspoon salt
½ head cabbage, sliced into ¼-inch strips
1 teaspoon Aleppo pepper or red pepper flakes
2 tablespoons bulghur
¼ cup water or vegetable broth

1. In a Dutch oven or a deep fry pan with a lid, heat the butter and olive oil to shimmering over medium-high heat. Add the onion and salt and sauté till translucent.
2. Add the cabbage, stir well, then stir in the pepper and bulghur.
3. Add the water, stir, and cover. Simmer on low heat for 20 minutes, stirring occasionally.

Serves 4

Four ❧

Little Syria

That flood of immigrants coming to America around the turn of the twentieth century contained a proportionately large number of Lebanese; so many, in fact, that historical demographers have compared Lebanon to Ireland in that both claim more countrymen living outside their borders than within.

Reasons for the Irish diaspora are fairly clear—the potato famine, the oppressive British landlord system. But why did so many Lebanese leave their homeland and come to America? All my growing up I kept hearing how that homeland—the littoral region of Bilad al-Sham—was "the most beautiful place in all the whole wide world," and so I assumed the reason we left was that we, like so many fellow migrants yearning to breathe free, were escaping tyranny.

Lebanon's Christian population dates back to apostolic times, and historically it had always looked to the West—first to Greece and Rome, then to France, and by my father's time, to America—so it made sense that to escape the domination of the Hamidian regime, the Lebanese would join in the great turn-of-the-century migrations to the New World. But when I questioned my father, who himself had lived under Ottoman rule, he simply chuckled and shook his head. So did his contemporaries, those *ibn Arab* I was taught to call "Uncle" out of respect for their age, who had also been part of those early waves of immigrants. I was surprised. Were they saying it *wasn't* political oppression that drove them and those other pioneers to board passage on ocean liners headed west?

Not at all! Many who made up the first waves were Christians, and in Lebanon, anyway, the Turks had been nowhere near as harsh on the Christians as on their Muslim subjects.

Okay then, why?

Why else? To make money!

The end-of-the-century crash of the Lebanese silk industry was only one of many indicators of the region's weakening economy. Steamship agents offering cheap passage to fill steerage holds were riding on donkey back up into the Lebanese hills, traveling from village to village with tales of America's streets of gold. The idea was never to move away to live your life and die in America. The idea, as my dad and my "uncles" explained it, was to shovel the gold from the American streets, to make a heap of money, and then return to live out your life like a pasha in the most beautiful country in the whole wide world.

But as things turned out, while some ended up moving back to the Old Country, most didn't. Freedom, prosperity, entrepreneurial energy, and perhaps the most compelling of all, the promise of upward mobility for your children and grandchildren—the American way of life had a way of getting to you. It is said, "America grasps you by the ankles of your children!" So, the majority of Lebanese émigrés remained here, and when they died it was here where their American children buried them.

➔➔➔

Shortly after debarkation in New York, my father followed word-of-mouth directions to the "Little Syria" neighborhood on Washington Street near Battery Park, a tenement community that featured Middle Eastern shops, cafés, and churches. There a newcomer could, without completely letting go of the security of familiar language and customs, begin to venture out to the greater America beyond. And for the majority of those first Lebanese immigrants—men and women alike—that venturing forth took the form of door-to-door peddling. Extended credit and supplies by fellow countrymen, these "hucksters," as my father called them, sold "notions" and "white goods" such as lace, thread, shears, buttons, embroidery, and tablecloths to rural housewives. Some traveled their routes by flivver trucks or horse and wagon, bearing the goods in steamer trunks, called *sendouks*, while others, like my dad, traveled "by shoe leather," carrying their wares in large, backpacklike wicker baskets called *kashishis*.

Although Baba would work many different jobs during his early years in America, it was door-to-door peddling that he credited for schooling him in this new country's language, its money, and many of its customs. As familiar and comforting as Little Syria may have been, the idea was never to stay there but to go out beyond its confines and work hard, to scrimp and to save, and as Baba liked to put it, to "pinch every nickel so the Indian squeals and the buffalo shits," until finally you had put away enough nickels to get off the road and open your own store.

"Be your own boss!" I heard it all my growing up. "The harder you work, the luckier you get," I heard too. And "In America, you make your *own* luck!"

➤ ➤ ➤

With their first success, those early immigrants beckoned to relatives back in the Old Country to follow, one sponsoring the next in what would eventually become known as the Great Chain Migrations. Little Syrias began springing up wherever groups of Lebanese set up shop— from New York City to Seattle, from St. Paul to Baton Rouge. Toledo, Ohio, where my father eventually settled, had a Middle Eastern enclave in its North End. In Chicago, so many Melchite Christians arrived from just the town of Zahlé that the area of South Franklin and Washtenaw was nicknamed "Little Zahlé." Dearborn, Michigan, a suburb of Detroit, could boast the largest Arabic-speaking population outside the Middle East.

The reason these enclaves were known as Little *Syrias*—and not Little *Lebanons*—was that back then not only were the Lebanese officially referred to as Syrians, they called themselves that, too, their most recent homeland being the Ottoman province named Greater Syria that also included modern-day Jordan, Palestine, and Israel. Lebanon itself would not officially gain identity as an independent nation until 1943.

Some of the turn-of-the-century arrivals also referred to themselves as *Turki*, or "Turks," having been registered at Ellis Island as coming from "Turkey-in-Asia." Dad liked to tell the apocryphal Thanksgiving-time story about a kind-hearted farmer who offers his hayloft to a stranded huckster on a cold November night. Early the next morning the peddler, new to this country and still learning English, grabs his *kashishi* and hightails it out of there when he overhears the farmer's wife tell her husband to go get the hatchet because it's time to kill the turkey!

➤ ➤ ➤

My father's sister, Aunt Yemnah, was family renowned as a master cook not only of our Middle Eastern fare but also of Western cuisine, which she learned from her housewife neighbors in the small northwest Ohio town of Bryan, where she settled with her husband, Nemer, in the mid-1890s. Her house was about an hour's drive from Toledo, and when we visited on Sundays, she would serve up such exotic dishes as leg of lamb with mint jelly, Yankee pot roast, or glazed ham and sweet potatoes. Her Thanksgiving turkey with chestnut stuffing was legendary among the cousins.

Although the recipe that follows shares similarities with the traditional Thanksgiving fare that Aunt Yemnah prepared, it is a version straight out of Little Syria. Like so many American recipes that entered our immigrant ovens, it went in Western and came out tasting somewhat Eastern too. What Kitchen Arabic is to American English, such recipes are to American cuisine—the original fusion cooking!

Deeq Habash Mihsheh
(Lemon Turkey with Dressing)

¼ pound (1 stick) butter, melted
2 lemons, zested and halved
1 teaspoon salt
½ teaspoon black pepper
1 turkey, about 12 to 13 pounds
1 medium onion, halved
2 bay leaves
1 teaspoon ground cinnamon
½ teaspoon allspice
½ teaspoon paprika
1½ teaspoons ground thyme
2 tablespoons pomegranate molasses
1 orange, zested then cut into chunks
¼ cup olive oil
2 cinnamon sticks
2 cups white wine

1. Heat the oven to 325°F. Mix butter with the lemon zest, salt, and pepper. Starting from the neck end of the turkey, work fingers under the skin and carefully lift and loosen the skin over the breast and tops of drumsticks. Spread the lemon butter under the skin, then pat the skin back into place. Put the onion halves, lemon halves, and bay leaves in the turkey cavity.

2. Mix cinnamon, allspice, paprika, and thyme with the pomegranate molasses, orange zest, and olive oil. Brush to cover the turkey breast. Put cinnamon sticks and orange chunks into the turkey cavity.

3. Place turkey, breast up, on a V-shaped rack in a 12-by-17-inch pan. Pour wine into pan. Roast in oven for 3 to 4 hours, until an instant-read thermometer inserted in the thigh registers 165°F. Rest the turkey, covered loosely with foil, for at least 30 minutes before serving. Reserve pan juices for the gravy.

THE GRAVY:

2 tablespoons butter
1½ tablespoons all-purpose flour
½ cup wine (sherry or marsala)
1½ cups chicken stock
Dollop of orange juice
Pinch of spice mix made of equal amounts of ground cinnamon, allspice, and paprika
Salt and black pepper, to taste

4. While the turkey is resting, put pan juices into a fat separator. Melt butter in a saucepan over medium flame, then while stirring, sprinkle in the flour, a little at a time. Cook and stir for a minute or so, then stir in the wine, stock, pan juices, orange juice, and a pinch of spice mix. Bring to a boil, then let simmer over a low heat for 15 minutes. Taste to adjust for salt and pepper.

➤ ➤ ➤

Heshwet Bulghur
(Cracked Wheat Dressing)

2 tablespoons butter
1 onion, diced small
1 tablespoon tahini
1 cup #3 bulghur
2 garlic cloves, minced
2 cups chicken stock
2 tablespoons dried parsley
1 tablespoon dried mint
1 cup minced cherry tomatoes
3 tablespoons toasted pine nuts

1. Melt the butter in a 2-quart saucepan over medium heat. Add onion, tahini, bulghur, and garlic. Stir until onion turns translucent and the bulghur takes on a golden color, about 3 to 4 minutes.
2. Add the stock, parsley, and mint. Stir. Reduce the heat, cover, and let simmer until totally cooked, about 40 minutes.
3. Stir in the cherry tomatoes and pine nuts, and serve as a dressing alongside the turkey.

➜ ➜ ➜

When it comes to side relishes for roast turkey, I think that not even cranberry sauce pairs better than the Armenian macerated dried fruit salad known as *mirkatan*. While it's not Lebanese, it does come from our neck of the woods. Also, it makes a tasty Sephardic version of haroseth for a Passover seder.

Armenian Mirkatan (or Persian Khoshab)
(Mélange of Macerated Dried Fruit)

1 cup dried apricots, chopped
½ cup raisins
2 cups mixture of any dried fruits (such as figs, pears, mango, prunes), chopped
1 teaspoon hot pepper flakes
1½ cups fragrant hot tea (such as Bengal Spice)
1 tablespoon vanilla extract
1 tablespoon rose water (or orange-blossom water)
3 tablespoons brandy
1 cup almonds, blanched
Zest of 1 orange
¼ cup pine nuts, toasted
½ cup pistachio nuts
½ cup pomegranate arils

1. Stir together all the dried fruits with hot pepper flakes in a nonreactive bowl and cover with hot tea. Set aside to cool.
2. Once it's cooled, add the vanilla extract, rose water, and brandy, and leave to macerate overnight.
3. Next day, pour off excess liquid that hasn't been absorbed. Stir in almonds and zest. Sprinkle with pine nuts, pistachios, and pomegranate arils, and serve.

Five

Ya Beladi, Ya Beladi . . .

In his early "huckster" years, my father and his fellow Syrian peddlers delighted in chance encounters on the road. *"Ibn Arab, inta?"* ("Are you a countryman?") they might call out, even to a total stranger, and for no other reason than whoever it was might happen to have dark eyes and hair, a golden cast to the skin, or a familiar accent. Camping out under the stars in rural Ohio, Michigan, Indiana, groups of peddlers would share a meal together, and if one of them had a jar of homemade arak to share, it wouldn't be long before the *atayba* singing would begin. Well, singing might not be the right word. *Atayba* isn't so much singing as it is a bluesy string of musical exclamations, pronouncements of joy, and long slow wails of longing, encouraged by cries of "Allah!" Listen to any soulful, rough-voiced flamenco singer—José Reyes for example—and you'll immediately recognize cante jondo's Arabic roots. After all, the Moors occupied Andalusian Spain for centuries, and the flamenco cry "Olé!" is a Spanish transliteration of "Allah!"

One of *atayba*'s most common themes is of homesickness and nostalgia for the old country, which in Arabic is called *il B'lad*. "Ya beladi, ya beladi," they would wail, "Oh my homeland, oh my homeland."

Homesickness is a spectrum. On the simple nostalgia end it's a vague discomfort, minor and fairly manageable. Warm at times, even rosy. But in the violet light, when you're making your way all by yourself along a foreign rural road, the pain focuses and becomes sharp. And remains unexpressed, since your only language is, "Thread today, missus? Scissors?"

During those months on the road, the closest thing my father had to home was the house of Yemnah and Nemer. So, when Baba finally had saved enough from peddling, it was in nearby Toledo that he opened a grocery and specialty butcher shop. A natural businessman, he prospered, eventually expanding to commercial real estate investments. He worked hard, but also people took to him. He was extroverted and charming, and he soon made influential friends in the local, Irish-dominated, Democratic machine. The Little Syria community's matchmakers saw this successful, eligible bachelor and got down to work. Before long a marriage was arranged for him to a young woman from Chicago, a second-generation *bint Arab* named Eva.

➤ ➤ ➤

My half-sister, Josephine, was the child of the union of Elias and Eva. Born in 1910, she would live to within a couple months of her hundredth birthday. A long life, and she was feisty and keen witted every minute of it. Always a good heart, she was a beloved grandmother and great-grandmother, a terrific cook (her *shish barak* recipe is legend among the Toledo families), and she was a wonderful storyteller. I interviewed her in 2008 for Samir Abu-Absi's award-winning book *Arab Americans in Toledo* and captured some of her reminiscences of the North End's Little Syria, like the time at the Daughters of Phoenicia ballroom above Hanf Drugs when she danced the Charleston to "The Twelfth Street Rag." Danny Thomas (back then he was still Amos Jacobs) sang at her engagement party, and when she was a young mother, Jameel Farah (a.k.a. Jamie Farr, *M*A*S*H*'s Klinger) lived next door and used to play with her son, Bobby. Here's one of Jo's stories from that interview, in her own words:

ME: What was Jamie Farr like as a kid?
JOSEPHINE: His mother was one of the most beautiful women I've ever seen in my life, but Jameel looks just like his father. I figured it had to have been an arranged marriage. Luckily, Jameel's sister took after her mother.

The people who lived downstairs from us then, her name was Goldie Cook, and her son was Joe Cook. Joe was older than Bobby, and Bobby adored him. He taught Bobby how to box because Jameel used to beat him up all the time. The lady that lived across the street from us, a Syrian lady, had just come home from the hospital where they treated tuberculosis patients, and for her health she had to sit in her front window in the sun, and so she'd sit there and watch the kids play. She liked Bobby and used to call him over and give him candy. But one day she told him if you don't hit Jameel back, I'm not going to give you candy anymore. And that's when Joe Cook taught Bobby how to box. Bobby got good at it. He started to take regular lessons and went on to join the Golden Gloves.

Joe Cook didn't like his new stepfather so when he was fifteen he lied about his age to join the service. He was at Pearl Harbor, the first Toledoan to die in World War II.

➤ ➤ ➤

Some claim that the following dish originated in Persia, the name devolving from ancient Farsi for "lamb's ear," presumably after the shape of the dumplings.

My Sister Jo's Shish Barak
(Stuffed Dumplings in Yogurt Sauce)

THE DUMPLINGS:
2 cups all-purpose flour, plus extra for dusting
Pinch of salt
Lukewarm water

THE FILLING:
½ medium onion, minced
1 teaspoon salt
1 tablespoon olive oil
¾ pound ground lamb
1 teaspoon black pepper
1 teaspoon ground cinnamon
2 teaspoons ground coriander

THE SAUCE:
3 tablespoons butter
2 garlic cloves, minced
1 tablespoon ground coriander
1 tablespoon dried ground mint
½ cup chopped fresh cilantro
6 cups plain yogurt
3 cups water (or chicken broth)
2 tablespoons arrowroot
3 ounces cold water
1 large egg
Juice of 1 lemon
¼ cup toasted pine nuts

1. Sift the flour into a bowl with pinch of salt. Gradually add water, a little at a time, and knead to obtain a soft dough that holds together and is smooth and shiny. Add a bit more flour or a tablespoon more water as needed. Knead the dough (or, as Jo's directions specify: "Slam it, punch it, hit it"). Cover the dough with a towel or plastic wrap and let it sit for 20 minutes.

2. Meanwhile, in a skillet, fry onion and salt in oil over medium heat until translucent (about 3 to 4 minutes); add meat to brown (4 to 5 minutes). Stir in pepper, cinnamon, and coriander (about 2 minutes), then set aside in a dish to cool.

3. With a rolling pin, roll the dough out "nice and thin" on a flour-dusted surface. Using a shot glass rim, cut into rounds. Place about ½ teaspoon filling in the center of each round, fold into a crescent and pinch together the edges, then pinch together the ends into a crescent shape similar to tortellini.

4. Heat butter in a small fry pan and sauté 2 garlic cloves, coriander, mint, and cilantro.

5. Pour yogurt into a Dutch oven and mix with water and stir until yogurt is dissolved. Turn heat to medium low and stir till it comes to a boil, then turn heat to low.

6. Mix arrowroot with 3 ounces cold water in a jar, shake well, and pour into a bowl. Add egg to the bowl and mix with a mixer. Starting with a little drizzle at a time, gradually temper the arrowroot mixture by pouring in a cup of hot yogurt from the Dutch oven, then pour all back into the Dutch oven.

7. Stir in the dumplings. Stir in the sautéed garlic mixture. Return to boil, then return to simmer, stirring regularly to keep dumplings from sticking together.

8. When dumplings turn white (about 15 to 20 minutes), it means the dough is done, and the *shish barak* is ready. Stir in lemon juice and remove from heat. Garnish with pine nuts.

Serves 8

Note: This recipe is for the soupy version; add less water if you prefer a thicker, more stewlike consistency for serving on rice.

Six

Kaan Makaan

During the years it took my father to save enough money to open his own store, he had worked not only as a huckster but at a number of other jobs as well. He was a short-order cook; a barber; a butcher; for a time he tramped the downtown streets wearing the boards of a full-length front-and-back sandwich sign advertising "Red Devil Potted Meats" (which gave him his first nickname in America, "the Red Devil"); he sold fruit from a pushcart—called a hokeypokey in those days; he was a counterman in a confectionery; and a city directory from the late nineteen aughts lists him as a "candy butcher and ice cream cone maker." A decade or so later, after the Volstead Act was passed, my father would begin earning money at an occupation you wouldn't find in any city directory—that of bootlegger.

Dad had become friendly with local politicians who ran Toledo's "Irish Combination" back in the early 1920s. These politicians knew people "who knew people" who put my father on the payroll to "help out a couple friends of friends" whose business happened to include delivering whiskey after it had been smuggled across Lake Erie from Canada. Dad's role was to keep a hotel room in downtown Toledo where the monthly shipments could be stored safely out of sight until they were picked up by the distributors. Who, by the way, were not from Detroit or Chicago as you might expect but from Kentucky of all places, the very home of fine bourbon! Dad said these distributors had a warehouse "right across the river from Cincinnati," where the liquor was doctored with water, grain alcohol, and malt for coloring. Diluted by as much as a third, it was rebottled and the corks reglued with counterfeit seals.

Remember *kaan makaan*, the Arab storyteller's "once upon a time"? Well, if any of my dad's stories ever rated a "maybe it happened, maybe it didn't," it would be this one. It's so much a boy story, with everything a boy could ask for—cops, smugglers, tough guys talking tough, even a punch in the mouth—that as a kid, I wanted to believe everything in it. Even today, as I write it down for the first time, the whole thing doesn't seem all *that* unbelievable. Especially considering my father's hot temper.

The story begins one evening as Baba was eating his supper in the kitchen of a Chinese restaurant next door to the hotel where he had a room rented for storing whiskey. Out of nowhere, someone grabbed his chair from behind, spun him around, and said, "Geha, you son of a bitch, where do you keep your stuff?" My father recognized the tall, square-shouldered man as a "dick"—Dad's old-timey term for "detective"—with the Toledo Police Department.

Telling me this part of the story, Baba's left eye would narrow and his jaw stiffen a little. My father was not a big guy, but he did have a big temper, and he certainly didn't like being called names. Returning the detective's curse with an Arabic one of his own, he leaped out of the chair, seized a meat cleaver hanging on the wall, and began swinging it. What was he thinking? That he could dash out the alley door and somehow make a getaway? If so, he didn't see the detective's partner behind him. Nor the uniformed policeman now coming at him with handcuffs. It turned out to be a full-fledged raid, as more policemen rushed into the back room to help the detectives subdue the crazy Syrian with the cleaver.

"After they got the handcuffs on me, they took me across the alley and up to my hotel room." It was a one-bedroom suite, meaning there was a smaller sitting room attached, and that was where the whiskey was. Cases of it. "I got 'em stacked from the wall out to the middle of the room." The detectives wanted to know where the rest of the stuff was kept. The rest of the stuff? How big an operation were they looking for? Dad answered, truthfully, that this was all of it. "But they don't wanna hear that."

Whenever Dad told this story, he would pause here to perform a little "let's get to work" pantomime imitation of the detective: dry-spitting into the palm of one hand then into the other, then briskly rubbing his hands together before coming up with fists.

The "questioning" continued on and off, into the evening. "They took turns," Dad said, providing sound effects by repeatedly smacking fist into palm. Finally, there came a knock at the door. Out in the hallway stood eight or ten "tall, red-faced Irishmen from downtown." One of them was a police inspector in plainclothes, two were lawyers, and the rest were muscle-bound goons in tight celluloid collars, but they were all connected to Toledo's Democratic machine, which at the time was run by my father's closest friend, Johnny O'Dwyer. "We hear you've got Geha," said one of the Irishmen, a lawyer from the city attorney's office.

"So what if we do?"

"We're assuming custody. That's so what." The lawyer showed a writ, held it high for all to see. Then putting out his other hand he crooked a forefinger. "Hand him over."

Dad told me the Irishmen drove him to St. Vincent's Hospital to have his nose set and his ribs taped, then to the Safety Building, where he was booked, fined, and "in a couple-three hours," released. Limping into his hotel room in the predawn gloom, he found that the cases of Canadian liquor hadn't even been confiscated.

That's it, end of story. I heard it from Baba a number of times, probably at my request, because I loved hearing it. He was an old man all the years I knew him, and I got to know him only after he was diminished by debilitating illness. I realize now that down deep I felt that I'd been cheated out of the kind of father that my friends had had. "Uncles" and older cousins spoke highly of my father, but always in terms of past glories: how daring E.E. had been! What business sense!

So, I loved the bootlegging story. *Kaan* or *makaan*, I didn't care. For me, it was bracing enough just to imagine a time when my father might have worn a pinstripe suit and a pinkie ring instead of a lamb-stained grocer's apron.

➤ ➤ ➤

One of Dad's favorite meals was a combo casserole he created out of two traditional egg-and-tomato dishes—a Lebanese *bayd bi benadora* (eggs with tomatoes) and a Tunisian *shakshuka* (egg-tomato casserole).

Dad's Bayd bi Benadora
(Tomato-Egg Casserole)

1 tablespoon butter
1½ tablespoons olive oil
1 medium onion, coarsely chopped
1 pound lamb shoulder or leg meat, cut into 1-inch cubes
2 garlic cloves, minced
1 tablespoon ground cinnamon
1 teaspoon allspice
½ teaspoon salt
½ teaspoon black pepper
1 cup water or chicken broth
1 can (14.5 ounces) diced tomatoes
4 large eggs
¼ cup chopped fresh cilantro

1. Using a large sauté pan, mix butter and oil and fry onions until translucent. Remove onions and set aside.
2. In the same pan, brown the lamb cubes in batches of several at a time.
3. Return the onions into the pan with the lamb. Stir in the garlic. Sprinkle with cinnamon, allspice, salt, and pepper.
4. Stir in the water with half the tomatoes, cover, and lower heat to a slow simmer for about 45 minutes.
5. Add the rest of the tomatoes.
6. Using the bottom of a large spoon, make 4 indentations in the stew and carefully break the eggs into the indentations. Sprinkle the cilantro over the eggs.
7. Cover and simmer over medium-low heat about 10 minutes or until the eggs are set. Serve with pita bread.

Serves 4

➜ ➜ ➜

This eggplant stew, another of Dad's creations, is one I found to be perfect for making in a slow cooker.

Beitenjahn Yaqnah
(Eggplant Stew)

1 can (14.5 ounces) stewed tomatoes
2 cups chicken broth
½ cup tomato paste
1½ pounds lamb (shoulder or leg), cut in cubes
1 large onion, diced large
2 teaspoons allspice, divided
2 tablespoons ground cinnamon, divided
½ teaspoon salt
1 teaspoon black pepper
3 to 5 garlic cloves, slivered
½ cup marsala wine
1 large eggplant
¼ cup extra-virgin olive oil
¼ cup all-purpose flour
2 teaspoons smoked paprika
Pine nuts and chopped parsley for garnish

1. Set slow cooker to high. Stir in stewed tomatoes, chicken broth, and tomato paste.
2. In a large fry pan, brown the lamb (working in batches). Remove and place in slow cooker.
3. In the same pan, sauté onion on medium high, 4 to 5 minutes or until they begin to turn translucent. Lowering the heat to medium, stir in 1 teaspoon of the allspice and 1 tablespoon of the cinnamon, as well as salt and pepper. Add the garlic, stir, let cook another 2 to 3 minutes.
4. Add spiced onion and garlic to the slow cooker. Deglaze the pan with marsala wine, and add to the slow cooker. Turn down slow cooker to low. Let cook 2 hours.
5. Meanwhile, preheat oven to 425°F. Peel and cut eggplant into 1½-inch cubes, sprinkle with salt, and let sit 20 minutes. Rinse and pat dry. Mix together the flour, the remaining 1 teaspoon of allspice, the remaining 1 tablespoon of cinnamon, and the paprika. Toss cubes in olive oil, then dust with the flour-spice mixture.

6. Place well-dusted eggplant cubes on a wire rack atop a cookie sheet and brown in oven (about 15 to 20 minutes, turning once).
7. Gently stir the eggplant into the slow cooker. Let cook another hour.

Serves 4 to 6 . . . with Riz bi Siriyeh (page 15)
or buttered egg noodles

➻ ➻ ➻

Peeling the eggplant is purely personal preference, since the skin is edible and contains many of the fruit's nutrients. Not only is the eggplant a fruit, it's actually a berry! For this reason, and because the female is seedier than the male, thus increasing the chances it might be bitter, you might want to check the sex of an eggplant before buying it. Seriously. This is an old greengrocer's technique: You discern an eggplant's sex by looking at its bottom, or blossom, end (opposite of the stem end), and if the indentation looks to be deep and more elongated than round, it's female; if the indentation is shallow and round, it's male, and the better choice.

Seven

Jiddo Mike

Baba wasn't the only bootlegger in the family, according to my cousin Mike Geha. Mike and I are cousins of some sort, but with my dad belonging to Mike's grandfather's generation, we never did figure out all the "once-removeds." Even so, it's no surprise that we became close friends: we're the same age—born two weeks apart—and we lived most of our growing up within walking distance of one another's houses; we attended the same schools, stocked shelves together at his dad's supermarket, and perhaps most important, we "got" one another. As teenagers we joked together about the same things, sharing a no bs outlook on the world that was at once earnest and ironic. Throughout most of our adult lives, Mike and I have lived in different parts of the country, but to this day we remain close friends and confidantes; at least a couple of times a week, he or I will pick up the phone to share a laugh, to hash over a problem, or as we age, simply to reminisce. Maybe even more than I do, Mike has always loved family stories, and he has a wealth of them. One of my favorites is about his *jiddo*, or "grandpa," also named Mike, and how as a young man back in Prohibition days, he was arrested for distilling arak. A clear-colored, anise-flavored liqueur similar to the Greek ouzo or the Turkish raki, arak might be called Lebanon's national drink. It's most often made from the muscat grape, and the best arak comes from the vineyards of Lebanon's northern Beqaa region, specifically the city of Zahlé. Because it's always been hard to find arak in America, basement stills had been turning out family recipes long before Prohibition. But even after the Volstead Act, it was no crime to distill small amounts of alcohol for home consumption; where the law stepped in was at large-scale manufacturing, distribution, and sale of the stuff. At the time of his arrest, Jiddo Mike had *three* stills in his basement! He'd always supported his growing family by peddling produce out of an old panel truck, but with Prohibition he'd apparently decided to widen his inventory a bit. There's no *kaan makaan* about this part of the story because my cousin has it in black and white, a clipping from the now long defunct *Toledo News-Bee*, which reported that "the deputy chief state prohibition inspector and his aides raided the home of Mike Geha, 838 Summit Street," where they found "50 gallons of Arak mash (crushed grapes) and Arak in a quart bottle."

But my cousin tells me that the newspaper didn't cover all there was to the story . . .

When Jiddo Mike's case came up in court, he pleaded guilty and was sentenced to a month in the Lucas County Jail. As it happened, the sheriff at the time knew Mike and liked him. He also liked "Syrian food," and it so happened that Mike's wife, H'naneh (in English, Anna, but to my cousin and me she was always Sittu, or "Grandma"), was one of the best cooks in the whole of north Toledo's Little Syria neighborhood—which in those days was saying something! So, according to the family story, Jiddo Mike and the sheriff came to an agreement: every evening after work, the sheriff would take Mike out of his jail cell in the downtown Safety Building and drive him the short distance to his house on Summit Street. There, the two of them would sit down together at the kitchen table, tuck a napkin into the front of their collars, and dig into a large, delicious meal served up by H'naneh. Then, after cigars and a shot or two of home-brewed arak (which the sheriff also favored), Mike would be left to spend the night in his own bed. Next morning a deputy on his way to work would stop by to pick Jiddo up and return him to his cell. This went on for the entire month of Jiddo Mike's sentence.

➵ ➵ ➵

The Phoenicians first used fermented date palms to distill the "national drink of Lebanon." The Arabic word *arak* means "sweat." In ancient times, as now, arak was stored in clay amphorae, which would "sweat" as they aged, promoting water evaporation and supposedly increasing the liquor's potency. Most arak sold in the United States is about 60 percent alcohol, or 120 proof. This makes it highly flammable and perfect for flambeau-style presentations, as in the following recipe.

Jibnet Miq'leh Beiruti
(Beirut-Style Fried Cheese)

1 pound Nablus cheese (or *kefalotyri* or Halloumi or kasseri—
   or even pecorino romano) cut in ½-inch-thick tiles of approximately
   1½ inches square.
½ cup of all-purpose flour with added black pepper, to taste
½ cup oil (¼ olive, ¼ grapeseed)
2 tablespoons arak, for flaming
2 or 3 lemons, quartered

1. Moisten each cheese slice with cold water and dredge in the flour.
2. In a small, heavy-bottomed fry pan (cast-iron works best), heat the oil
   over medium-high heat and sear each slice until golden-brown on both
   sides.
3. For added drama, sprinkle with gently warmed arak and set afire with a
   fireplace match. (Oopah!)
4. Serve hot with a last-minute squeeze of fresh lemon juice and with ouzo
   or arak on the side with briny olives and crusty bread.

Serves 6

Tip: Nablus cheese, along with the other suggested varieties, are available
online or at Middle Eastern markets.

➨ ➨ ➨

Traditionally, arak is served as an aperitif, in a thin, narrow glass. Like its
cousins, the Greek ouzo and the Turkish raki, adding ice and a little water will
turn the liquor from clear to the milky-white drink known in the Middle East
as "lions' milk." But be sure to add the ice *after* the water, because adding ice
before the water causes a film to develop on the surface of the arak. The film
(sometimes manifesting as tiny frosty-looking flakes) doesn't affect the flavor
of the arak, just the appearance, but to a fussy guest it might look like you
don't know what you're doing. Which, in a culture so heavily steeped in hospitality (not to mention concern for what others will say), is just not a good
thing.

Rarely drunk by itself, arak is usually an accompaniment to *maza*, which is
pretty much a deluge of small-dish appetizers. At home a *maza* might include
four, five, even six or more dishes—anything from kibbeh (both raw and
sautéed in patties), *suf-souf* salad, hummus, baba ghanoush, and maybe some
jibneh cheese and briny olives. But a restaurant *maza*—as I discovered at the

Kit Kat Club in Beirut when I visited there back in 1971—can go to two dozen or more dishes, from marinated baby eggplants stuffed with walnuts to lamb brain in scrambled eggs, which I loved at first bite but couldn't finish when I discovered what it was. Sometimes it's best just not to ask.

Suf-Souf
(Tabouli Salad)

¾ cup #2 bulghur
¾ cup orange juice
2 bunches curly leafed parsley, finely chopped
½ cup scallions, finely chopped
3 medium tomatoes, seeded, diced small
1 cup mint leaves, chopped
1 garlic clove, crushed and chopped
1½ tablespoons crushed dried mint
1 teaspoon allspice
1 teaspoon salt
½ teaspoon black pepper
Juice of 3 lemons
¼ cup olive oil, plus more for serving
Romaine or grape leaves for serving

1. Place bulghur in a small bowl, cover with orange juice, and let soak 15 minutes. Squeeze excess juice out of the bulghur with your hands, then combine bulghur and all remaining ingredients in a large bowl and mix well.
2. Best to chill 1 hour or 2 in the fridge, then drizzle with a little extra olive oil before serving.
3. Serve mounded on a platter of romaine leaves or grape leaves that have been well rinsed or blanched a minute or so in hot water. The dish can be eaten with a fork, like a salad, but encourage your guests to use the leaves to scoop up bites of *suf-souf.*

Tip: For nonclumpy results, better to hand-chop the parsley rather than use a food processor.

➤ ➤ ➤

A TRICK FROM AN OLD-TIMEY BOOTLEGGER

There's a recipe tip, or "kitchen hack," that came out a couple years ago in *Cook's Illustrated Magazine* that involves dosing a bottle of cheap whiskey with 1 tablespoon of dry sherry, ⅛ teaspoon of liquid smoke, and ½ teaspoon of vanilla. Simple. I've tried it, and the trick sort of works, although some may not like the liquid smoke taste (I didn't). But rather than fiddle with the recipe, here's an older, even simpler trick from my Dad's Prohibition years: Simply pour a single shot of port wine into a bottle of cheap whiskey and give the bottle a shake. Too simple? What have you got to lose?

Eight 🦎

The Full Catastrophe

When portraying your own family there can be the temptation to gloss over foibles or enhance the positive qualities, especially if you find your people so appealing to begin with. The fact that they are a Mediterranean people, complete with an inborn capacity for an emotional range straight out of high opera, well that's just part of the territory. My father, for example, could be passionately angry at you one minute and the next minute charming you with a canny, self-directed humor.

It was only a few months after my dad died that the movie *Zorba the Greek* came out. I was just nineteen then, a young nineteen, and maybe that's why I was so struck by the resemblance I saw between my father and Anthony Quinn in the role of Zorba. I felt the similarity to be so remarkable that I came back to the theater again a couple nights later, and as I sat there watching and listening, I remember wondering whether somehow, someway, it could have been possible that Anthony Quinn had actually met my father and studied him for the role. A crazy notion, of course, so I didn't say anything to anybody. But soon people who'd known my father—cousins, neighbors, childhood friends I'd grown up with—saw the movie and mentioned the amazing resemblance. And the similarity wasn't just in physical looks—although that alone astounded us—but in attitude as well. Even down to the minor mannerisms Quinn adopted for the role!

And yet, just as I couldn't deny feeling some pride to hear my friends detail the similarities between my grocer father and Kazantzakis's earthy, passionate, mad-for-life hero embodied in Anthony Quinn, I also couldn't deny my own private, deflating observation: poor Mrs. Zorba and the kids. Colorful characters are fun to read about or to watch on the screen, but to live with? Not so much. Even Zorba himself refers to his experience with marriage and family life as "the full catastrophe."

Like Zorba, Dad married young the first time, to Eva, when he was twenty-one. A year later, in 1910, his first child, Josephine, was born.

My half-sister, Jo, was always strong willed, even as a youngster. Judging by the old photographs, she looked like she'd begun her teenaged years as a Gibson Girl and ended them as a flapper, when at age nineteen, she fell in love and decided to put the Roaring Twenties behind her and settle down with Alex, the man of her dreams.

Dad, however, was dead set against the whole thing. But why? The groom-to-be was not only age appropriate and employed, he was also a fellow *ibn Arab* from north Toledo's Little Syria neighborhood. Nevertheless, Baba disapproved of Alex. Maybe he knew something nobody else knew. Or maybe the custom back then being that parents arranged a daughter's marriage, it was simply a case of Old Country tradition clashing head-on with newfound American freedom. Whatever the reason, Baba was adamant. But if he could be stubborn, so could his daughter. Jo's mother, Eva, sided with her, and long story short (insert here months of yelling, of pleading, of slammed doors and shouts down, of screaming matches and teeth-grinding slow burns), Baba gave up arguing. Keeping his own counsel, he decided, like Zorba, to go off and leave this "full catastrophe" behind him.

In March 1929, under the pretense of setting up a business arrangement with an East Coast importer of Turkish rugs, he boarded the Lake Shore Limited for New York. Back in Toledo, word arrived that he'd embarked on a ship for Beirut. Then it was discovered that he'd cleaned out the family savings. He did leave Eva and Josephine something—the store, a couple minor real estate holdings—but the real money, a sizeable nest egg they had both worked to build up over the years, had disappeared along with him.

It was early April by the time Dad's ship arrived in Beirut. Right away, he got down to business and put his money to work, opening what would, in a few months' time, become a successful feed and grain store. Unbeknownst to his family back in the States, he also had engaged the services of a matchmaker, and just as the 1930s were dawning, he'd made arrangements to meet my mother.

➤➤➤

Back when my father was boarding that ship in New York, bound for Beirut, he had an unusual encounter. As he was going up the departures side of the gangway, a fashionably dressed young woman who happened to be passing on the other—or arrivals—side of the railing caught his eye. He immediately felt drawn to her as if he knew her. Then he felt a shiver when she, too, looked over at him and they briefly locked eyes. She was young, a teenager, and a perfect stranger. After passing one another on the crowded gangway, each once more glanced back at the other. It was a moment that neither would ever forget. Nearly two decades later they would meet again, and each would recall this moment in mutual amazement. The young woman was my aunt Sophie, coming to America to join her two sisters who had arrived here earlier. Dad knew that in the years after he'd run away from home, his father and stepmother had had three daughters, but he'd never seen his half-sister Sophie before that moment on the gangway, much less known that she was coming to America.

➤ ➤ ➤

Over the years this story of a remarkable coincidence became one we often heard around the Sunday table, either at our house or at Aunt Sophie's up in Detroit. And this is one of my favorites of her recipes that she brought with her to America.

Fasoulia
(Aunt Sophie's White Bean Stew)

2 cans (14.5 ounces) cannellini beans, drained and rinsed (or 2 pounds dried cannellini beans soaked overnight in water to cover and 1 heaping tablespoon of baking soda)
1½ tablespoons olive oil
1 pound lamb (leg or shoulder), cut into ¾-inch cubes
8 to 12 garlic cloves, chopped
½ cup tomato paste
1 tablespoon ground cinnamon
1 teaspoon allspice
1 teaspoon ground coriander
½ teaspoon salt
¼ teaspoon black pepper
1 bunch cilantro, chopped, divided
¼ cup lemon juice

1. Boil the beans in water to cover for 15 minutes.
2. Meanwhile, heat the olive oil to shimmering in a large fry pan or Dutch oven, then add the lamb to brown.
3. Stir in garlic and tomato paste, sauté for a minute or so.
4. Stir in cinnamon, allspice, coriander, salt, and pepper.
5. Carefully drain the beans and add to the meat mixture.
6. Add all but a generous sprinkle of the cilantro, add lemon juice, stir, and remove from heat.
7. Garnish with the remaining sprinkle of cilantro and serve with Riz bi Siriyeh (page 15).

Serves 4 to 6

➼ ➼ ➼

Mjedderah, another dish that Aunt Sophie made, happens to be among the most ancient of dishes. In Middle Eastern Jewish tradition it's nicknamed "Esau's Favorite" because it's claimed to be Jacob's "mess of pottage" that smelled so good his elder brother, Esau, traded his birthright just for a bowlful of the stuff.

It's also one of the first recipes I demoed at Cooks' Emporium, a kitchen store in downtown Ames, Iowa, where several times a year for over two decades, I presented cooking demonstrations of Middle Eastern cuisine. In fact, it was the audiences at those Saturday morning demos who first suggested I collect my recipes in a cookbook and to be sure and include the kind of family stories I related while waiting for the onions to caramelize!

Speaking of caramelized onions, that's where *mjedderah* gets its hearty flavor, and the high protein content of its lentil and rice combo makes it a nutritious substitute for meat. Raised an Old-Country Catholic, I must have eaten *mjedderah* every single Friday of my childhood.

The word *mjedderah* defies pronunciation by non-Arabic speakers. Here's my best attempt as I tried to break it down for my Cooks' demo audience: start by making an *m* sound but don't finish the *m*, quickly jump to a *j* sound; shorten the *e* and roll the *d* into the *r* with a quick French-like roll right up to the final *ah* sound. *Mmm-jeh-drr-ah!*

Luckily, *mjedderah* is much easier done than said. Here's how . . .

Mjedderah
(Lentil Pottage)

1½ cups brown or green lentils
6 cups water (or chicken broth for nonvegetarian version)
½ teaspoon salt
1 medium onion, diced
½ cup olive oil, divided
½ teaspoon black pepper
½ teaspoon ground coriander
¼ teaspoon ground cumin (optional)
¼ teaspoon cayenne pepper (optional)
½ cup short-grained rice
1 large onion, halved then sliced into crescents

1. Wash lentils. Bring water and salt to boil in Dutch oven and add lentils.
2. Cover and cook 15 minutes over medium heat.
3. Meanwhile, using a fry pan, brown diced onion in ¼ cup of the olive oil (10 to 12 minutes).
4. In the last 2 minutes of browning, add pepper and coriander to onions, and if desired, add cumin and cayenne.
5. Add browned onions and rice to lentils, stir, and cover.
6. Let cook 25 to 30 minutes longer over medium-low heat.
7. While lentils and rice cook, sauté large onion crescents in the remaining ¼ cup of oil until golden brown. (The deeper brown, the sweeter, as the onions caramelize; but if you go beyond golden-brown, keep stirring!)
8. Remove onions with slotted spoon and set aside; pour a couple tablespoons of the onion-infused oil into the cooked lentils and rice. Stir.
9. Ladle the pottage onto a platter. It will thicken as it cools. Top with sautéed onions and a tablespoon or so of the oil.

Variation: Substitute bulghur for rice, add 10 minutes to boiling time.

Serves 8 . . . with pita bread and toppings

SUGGESTED TOPPINGS
1 cup crumbled feta cheese
1 cup mix of chopped tomato and chopped scallions
¼ cup chopped fresh cilantro or Italian parsley
and/or
- a sprinkling of chopped hot banana peppers
- chopped beets and cabbage marinated overnight in 2 tablespoons lemon juice, 1 tablespoon olive oil, and ¼ teaspoon sugar

- chopped cabbage, onion, and dried mint marinated overnight in lemon juice, olive oil, and sugar

TRADITIONAL GARNISH
Chilled radishes
Lifit Ma'bous (recipe follows)

➤ ➤ ➤

Although *mjedderah* can be served hot, it's mostly eaten at room temperature. The perfect go-with is a plate of crunchy *lifit ma'bous*.

Lifit Ma'bous
(Pickled Turnips)

2 pounds turnips
3 tablespoons salt, divided
2 fresh beets (or ½ can [14.5 ounces] of sliced beets)
3 cups boiled water, cooled to lukewarm
¾ cup white vinegar
1½ teaspoons sugar

1. Peel and cut turnips into wedges. Toss in 1½ tablespoons of the salt and let sit in a colander for several hours, preferably overnight. Next day, rinse and drain.
2. Parboil, peel, and slice fresh beets into thin rounds or wedges. Or if using canned sliced beets, drain, reserving the liquid and including it as part of the 3 cups of water.
3. Pack turnips into 3 clean 2-pint jars in alternating layers with 3 or 4 slices of beets.
4. Mix together water, vinegar, sugar, and the remaining 1½ tablespoons of salt. Pour mixture into each jar to cover turnips, keeping about a ¼ inch or so of air. Seal tightly. Let sit a day or so on the counter, away from light. Then store in fridge. Ready to eat in about a week. Four days if you can't wait.

Note: If you like, you can add small wedges or strips of cabbage to the jars, cauliflowerets, peeled garlic (whole or sliced), or peppers.

The contents of the jars will turn a deep ruby red as they sit there on the kitchen counter, a warm and familiar sight, promising a taste of home.

Nine

Cigars and Yankee Dollars

My mother, Carmen Akel, was born in the Christian Quarter of Damascus, in the neighborhood called Bab Tuma. Her father, who worked as a bricklayer, took enormous pride in having helped restore an ancient church built against that part of the city wall where, tradition has it, Saint Paul was lowered in a basket to escape his persecutors. It's good my grandfather took such pride, since his salary didn't provide much more than that. Times were hard, and they would turn even harder after 1913, the year my mother was born the ninth of eleven children: the world war would open the way to political upheaval throughout the Middle East, and after it would come economic recessions, famine, and pandemics of typhus, typhoid fever, and the 1918 flu. Adding to the Akel family's financial burden was the fact that eight of the eleven children were girls: this in a culture that looked on female children as burdens, each needing to be provided a dowry before she could be married off by matchmakers.

What poorer families had to do in those days was to seek out suitors with already-established livelihoods. A few of these were widowers, but most were simply older bachelors looking to reclaim the youth they had spent pursuing their fortunes in the United States or South America. Financially well-off, they had no need of a dowry and were, in fact, happy enough to pay the matchmaker's fee themselves. Still, it was *ayb*, Mama would add, "shameful," the way so many of the Akel daughters were sold off to old men.

My mother's favorite uncle, Alexios, a Catholic priest of the Melchite Rite, approached the family when it was Mama's turn to be married. An abbot of a nearby monastery had informed him of a countryman who'd recently returned from America. A bachelor, the abbot said, who was looking to marry. So it was through Father Alexios that the matter was brokered. The year was 1931. Baba was forty-three, and the girl who was to become my mother was eighteen.

At their first meeting, Baba wore a stylish suit and he carried a fine fedora hat in his hand. He'd struck it rich, after all, like so many others who'd come back, smoking their fat cigars and giving away American silver dollars as if they were candy treats. The Akels laid out the traditional Arabic coffee and *ka'ak* cookies for his visit. As Father Alexios made the introductions, the Akels learned that since returning from America, their guest had started up a feed and grain business in nearby Zahlé, just across the Syrian-Lebanon border. They also learned that he was, like them, a Melchite Catholic. What they hadn't yet learned—not my mother nor her parents, nor Father Alexios—was that he had been married before, and that he was, in fact, still married.

→ → →

When guests stop by for a visit, formal or not, hospitality requires you to offer them a little something sweet to eat, like these simple but delicious cookies, and a little something to drink as well—coffee or tea, or if the weather is warm, maybe lemonade.

Ka'ak Sumsoum
(Sesame Cookies)

THE COOKIE DOUGH:
1 cup rendered butter
1¼ cups sugar
5 teaspoons baking powder
2 eggs (unbeaten)
6 drops anise oil
6 cups all-purpose flour
1 cup milk

THE TOPPING:
1 egg, well beaten
1 drop anise oil
½ cup sesame seeds, toasted

1. Preheat oven to 350°F.
2. Mixing ingredients by hand, blend together butter and sugar, add baking powder, eggs, and anise oil. As you begin to knead, gradually add some flour and some milk, alternating, a bit more flour, then a bit more milk, and so on until all ingredients are mixed in and well kneaded.
3. Divide dough into pieces the size of golf balls and roll each in the palms of your hands until it's about 4 inches long. Bring its ends together to form a ring.
4. Mix topping ingredients together in a shallow bowl. Dip each cookie so as to cover its top, then place it on an ungreased cookie sheet.
5. Place cookie sheet in the center of the oven and bake until lightly browned (approximately 15 to 20 minutes).

Makes about 50 cookies

➤ ➤ ➤

A single ingredient makes Arabic coffee Arabic—as opposed to Turkish: a touch of cardamom.

Ahweh
(Arabic Coffee)

1½ cups water (about ¼ cup per demitasse)
1 tablespoon sugar (about ½ teaspoon per demitasse)
2 tablespoons of Turkish—or pulverized—coffee (about 1 teaspoon per demitasse)
¼ teaspoon ground cardamom

1. Bring water to boil in an *ibrik* (Turkish coffee pot) if you have one, or in a small saucepan if you don't.
2. Add sugar. Stir. Add coffee, one spoonful at a time, stirring, then the cardamom. Return to boil.
3. The coffee will froth up. When this happens, remove from heat and spoon a little of the froth into each demitasse. Return to boil and let it rise and fall two more times (for a total of three times), each time spooning a little of the froth into the demitasses. Pour coffee into each demitasse and serve.

Makes 6 demitasse cups (4 ounces each)

Note: Coffee that is specially ground for Arabic coffee is available online and at Middle Eastern markets.

➤ ➤ ➤

Mighlee
(Syrian Tea)

8 cups water
½ cup anise seed (*yensoun*)
3 slices ginger, ½ inch thick
3 pieces *koulanjan* (galangal) (optional)
5 cinnamon sticks, whole

Place all ingredients into a saucepan and boil for 30 to 40 minutes. Serve with sugar.

➔ ➔ ➔

Limonada
(Syrian Lemonade)

1½ cups sugar
Juice of 6 to 7 lemons
1½ cups mint leaves, rinsed
1½ teaspoons orange-blossom water

1. Boil 1 cup water and stir in sugar till dissolved. Let cool.
2. In a pitcher stir together cooled sugar solution, lemon juice, mint, orange-blossom water, and 1½ quarts water. Chill with ice and serve.

➔ ➔ ➔

Ahweh Ubyid
(White Coffee)

Ahweh ubyid is nice to sip in the evening when you don't want to deal with caffeine. It's also fun for little kids who want to drink from a demitasse like the grown-ups.

1½ cups water
1½ teaspoons orange-blossom water, divided
6 teaspoons sugar, divided

1. Bring water to boil.
2. Into each of 6 demitasse cups add ¼ teaspoon of the orange-blossom water and 1 teaspoon of the sugar.
3. Fill each demitasse with boiling water and stir.

Makes 6 demitasse cups

Ten

Grass Widow

The term *grass widow* dates to Shakespeare's time, when it meant an unmarried woman who'd had a number of lovers. But language is always changing, and by the early 1800s the term had come to mean a wife who is abandoned for a newer one. In pioneer America, more than a few women were made into grass widows as their husbands left them behind to forge ahead into the American wilderness. Out there, so far from the log cabins or sod houses they once called home, many of these husbands took American Indian wives, who in turn also became grass widows after the men, continuing to push on toward the receding frontier, deserted them as well. A century later, during the pioneer days of the Great Migrations, the term *grass widow* once again made a brief appearance in common usage.

My father wasn't the only man to leave a grass widow, nor was he unusual in assuming that here is here and there is there and never the twain shall meet. He was wrong, of course—and on so many levels.

➤➤➤

The shocking news arrived shortly after my parents were married, traveling by way of the immigrant grapevine: *Back in America, Elias Geha was already legally married!* And just like that, my mother's world collapsed. Now *Ayb*, or "shame," had befallen her and all the Akel family. In those days and in that culture, *Ayb* (with a capital *A*) had an impact that went beyond embarrassment or shame; it was catastrophic disgrace.

While I was growing up, my mother's ordeal remained a family secret, something to be kept from the children. Over the years I heard allusions to it, more or less veiled, but I didn't know the full story until decades after Baba had died; even then, Mama told it to me hesitantly, reluctantly, as if still tender to the pain and the humiliation. But as for me, looking at it through what nowadays we call a modern lens, I was struck by the irony that my mother and Baba's first wife, Eva—the only persons completely innocent of any deception—were the ones who bore the brunt of public dishonor. In those times, only one recourse remained open to the Akels: Mama had to leave her new home in Zahlé and return to live with her family in Damascus.

There she remained in her parents' house, adrift in a kind of social limbo—married but not married. Her family, burdened with other daughters to marry off, reluctantly adjusted to having once again another mouth to feed. They were that poor. Decades later when Mama told me this story, her voice broke explaining how she could feel her mother's eyes on her at the dinner table, monitoring the portions she took.

Meanwhile Baba, left to his own devices, hooked up with a mistress (a cousin named Rasheedeh) and adopted the bachelor high life of a successful businessman. Things were different for men.

➤➤➤

After eight years, Eva—Dad's grass widow in America—developed pneumonia and died. When this news reached the Old Country, the abbot who'd acted as matchmaker was exposed for having taken a bribe to pronounce my father's first marriage "annulled." Furthermore, the Melchite synod was threatening the abbot with punishment, both civil and ecclesiastical, if things were not set right. The news of Eva's passing also caused Mama's family to begin urging that she return to her marriage. "Consider it a martyrdom" was how her priest-uncle, Alexios, had put it, a sacrifice that would lift from the Akels all these years of *Ayb*.

In Zahlé, meanwhile, Baba was also being pressured to "do the right thing" and take Mama back. So after eight years of separation, my father and mother agreed to reunite. Why? Mama felt dispossessed by her own family, steeped as they all were in a culture that looked on women in her situation as damaged goods. As for Baba, maybe he felt guilty, but more likely the thing with his cousin-mistress, Rasheedeh, had fizzled out by then. Whatever the reasons, my parents were rejoined after nearly a decade of separation and were once again recognized by both church and state as a legally married couple.

During that entire first year after Mama returned to his house in Zahlé, Baba proceeded to punish her, taking out on her the resentment he'd built up during their separation. But why, I wondered, if he felt that way, did he even take her back? My mother and I were at the kitchen table, and I was hearing these things for the first time. Mama's response was simple and direct: because a woman had had the audacity to leave him, a woman had exposed him and thwarted his plans. And now this woman was once again under his thumb. So he pressed down, treating her like his slave, punishing her with humiliation and physical abuse. As she told me this, Mama didn't go into many details, nor did I ask for them. It's hard to know some things about your own father. One specific, however, did emerge: how during that first year he would lock her up in a room for days at a time. I was reminded of the way my father's stepmother had treated him; what's done to us, we sometimes do to others.

➤ ➤ ➤

Soon after they were together again, Mama became pregnant. When VeeVee was born, Baba was disappointed that Mama had given him a daughter. He stomped out of the house and, according to the story, did not come back for two weeks. After he did return, however, he began to change. It seemed to happen quickly. One day he was furious that his firstborn was female, and then the next day the child was the apple of his eye. Simple as that. Then, while VeeVee was a toddler, Mama gave birth to my brother, Aboody. And Baba was delighted. In celebration, he filled a basket with coins and candies and invited the neighborhood children to reach in and take all they could grasp. I was born a year afterward, in 1944. Baba, who was fifty-six that year, couldn't have been happier.

It was we children, Mama claimed, who had saved her life.

Starting a second family seemed to have initiated a profound transformation in Baba. He felt a renewed pride that deepened with the birth of each of us. Looking back, I do believe the sincerity of his change of heart. My father was never an easy man to live with, but all my life I never for one second doubted what he felt for me, my brother, or my sister. We were loved, and we knew it. He claimed that we were the reason that he returned to America, thinking to improve our chances in life. Every day I am grateful to him for bringing us to America.

But his plans for doing so were interrupted by World War II. When the war began, Lebanon had been under the control of the Vichy French government. Although the territory was freed in 1941 by Allied forces, travel remained restricted for the duration of hostilities. Not until 1946 did general shipping reopen in the Mediterranean, and my parents—along with my sister (sick with typhoid!), my brother, and I—boarded the *Vulcania*, the first passenger ship after the war leaving Beirut harbor, taking us to a new life in America. A new world.

➤ ➤ ➤

There is an Arabic word—*ma'loub*—for when things flip and your world turns upside down. It's also the word from which this recipe derives its name. A nonvegetarian version of *ma'loubi* substitutes shredded strips of precooked (roasted or steamed) chicken breast for the eggplant. Another variation layers lima beans between the eggplant and the rice. Either way, this dish not only blends a myriad of different flavors and textures, it also provides the host or hostess one of the prettiest of presentations.

Ma'loubi
(The Upside-Down Dish)

1 eggplant
Salt
2 tablespoons olive oil
½ red bell pepper
¼ cup pine nuts
2 cups cooked Riz bi Siriyeh, spiced (see note below)
2 tablespoons chopped fresh cilantro

1. Slice eggplant into 3-by-2-inch tiles, salt, and let sweat for 20 minutes. Rinse and pat dry. Sauté in oil 3 minutes on a side, or till golden. Set aside to drain on paper towels.
2. Cut red pepper into 3-inch-long matchsticks. Set aside.
3. Toast the pine nuts in a single layer in the tray of a toaster oven. (Keep your eye on them!)
4. Preheat oven to 375°F. Grease a 10-inch cake pan. Cut a circle of parchment paper to fit inside the bottom of the cake pan. Spray the parchment paper with cooking spray.
5. To arrange the dish:
   a. Place the pine nuts in the center of the parchment paper so they roughly form a central disk.
   b. Place the red pepper sticks around the pine nut disk like spokes on a wheel.
   c. Layer the eggplant tiles atop the red pepper spokes in a circle like overlapping shingles.

d. Spread the Riz bi Siriyeh over the eggplant until the cake pan is full and press it down.

   e. Cover with foil.

6. Heat in oven for 30 minutes. Remove foil. Place serving platter over cake pan, invert. Tap around lightly with a spoon, then carefully lift cake pan. Carefully remove circle of parchment paper and ... voilà! Sprinkle with chopped cilantro and serve.

Note: To the Riz bi Siriyah recipe (page 15) stir in 1½ tablespoons chopped parsley, 2 teaspoons ground cinnamon, and 1 teaspoon ground allspice.

As a go-with, I like to serve a platter of Siliq Migleh.

Siliq Migleh
(Sautéed Swiss Chard)

THE DRESSING:
2 tablespoons lemon juice
3 tablespoons extra-virgin olive oil
1 garlic clove, crushed and minced
Pinch of sugar
¼ teaspoon salt
¼ teaspoon black pepper
Pinch of dried mint
1 tablespoon of tahini (optional)

THE CHARD:
1 bunch (about 1 pound) of Swiss chard (white or red)
6 tablespoons olive oil, divided
Crushed ice
1 medium onion, chopped
1 teaspoon salt
2 garlic cloves, minced

THE TOPPING:
1 large onion, sliced into thin crescents
3 tablespoons olive oil
1 lemon, cut into wedges

1. Whisk together all dressing ingredients and set aside.
2. Wash chard, cut/shred the leaves away from the thickest stems, and dice the stems. Set stems aside.

3. Heat 3 tablespoons of the olive oil in a Dutch oven; sauté the leaves over medium-high heat for about 2 minutes, stirring.
4. Remove from Dutch oven and let drain a moment or two in a colander. Meanwhile, fill a 1-gallon plastic bag halfway with crushed ice and seal.
5. Using kitchen tongs, spread the chard leaves on a platter, lay the bag of crushed ice over them, and place the platter into the freezer to shock and stop cooking.
6. After 5 minutes, remove from freezer and place chard in a large bowl.
7. Heat the remaining 3 tablespoons of the olive oil in the Dutch oven and throw in the chopped onions, salt, and chard stems and sauté at medium-low heat until liquid is evaporated, the stems soften, and the onions begin to brown, about 8 to 10 minutes. During the last 2 minutes, add garlic.
8. Remove from heat and toss in the large bowl with the now cooled sautéed leaves. Sprinkle with dressing and place in fridge.
9. Sauté onion crescents in olive oil over medium heat until dark brown and crispy.
10. Bring the chard to room temperature before serving. Layer crispy browned onions on top. Garnish with lemon wedges.

Eleven

Enwhaddyelse?

Our first home in America was an apartment above my father's grocery store on Monroe Street, in Toledo's near-downtown. As a small boy, I had my parents to myself on school days, in the absence of my brother and sister. Upstairs, I loved "helping" Mama do her day-to-day chores, wiping down the enamel-topped kitchen table or drying silverware; downstairs, I'd sit perched on a stool behind the meat counter, swinging my legs and swatting at flies as I watched Baba carve up a shoulder of lamb, the ample belly of his apron smeared with red horizontal lines where he'd leaned against the butcher block. There, amid the smell of raw meat and of fresh sawdust on the floor, I remember how he'd pause now and again to resharpen his black-iron knife, eyes fixed in a distant, thoughtful gaze, while his hands rhythmically ran the quick up-and-back ring and scree of the blade against the honing steel. Thinking of what? I had no idea. As for me, I was content to simply stare off and imagine fire engines, Hopalong Cassidy, sword fights, and Superman.

➤➤➤

In the days before the widespread appearance of self-service shopping, small neighborhood groceries operated according to a protocol that went something like this: Whenever the screen door opened and slapped shut, Baba would put down his knife and sharpening steel, wipe his hands on the stomach of his apron, and come around the small meat case to wait on the customer. As the housewife recited the items on her list, my father would roam about the little store retrieving them for her, one by one. I remember a broomsticklike gadget he kept near the cash register. It had a pair of curved metal "fingers" on one end, which he used to clamp a can and bring it down off a high shelf. Placing each item on the counter, he would ask "Enwhaddyelse, Missus?" and she would glance at her list and tell him what else she wanted—a box of laundry soap or a pound of lunch meat. I loved watching the thin slices of salami fall onto the square of waxed paper in his hand as the electric slicer shushed back and forth. Wrapping the meat in brown butcher paper, then tying the package together with string from a large cone that hung above the cash register, he would place his hands flat on the counter, lean forward, smile: "Enwhaddyelse?"

➤➤➤

Enwhaddyelse had to have been the first English any of us ever learned; we heard it enough times. That, and its corollary, *Fine business,* became our family's expletives of choice, used interchangeably for exasperation or disbelief: Did the landlord finally come over and fix the leaky toilet? *Enwhaddyelse?* And now it's leaking again? *Fine business!* Did we drop by for a Sunday visit to a relative's house only to find them, by pure coincidence, getting into their car to come visit us? *Enwhaddyelse?* And by further coincidence they were bringing us a tin container of Turkish delights, exactly like the one we were bringing them? *Fine business!*

Speaking of coincidence—and we must, after all, this is real life, which unlike fiction is replete with coincidence—shortly after arriving in America and settling above the store on Monroe Street, we learned that Mama's eldest sister, Maheeba, who had long before married and left Damascus for America, lived only a short bus ride from us, up in Mount Clemens, Michigan, just past Detroit. And living in Detroit itself, an even bigger coincidence, was Baba's half-sister Sophie, whom he'd first encountered that day on the gangplank, all those years ago when she was just arriving in America as he was leaving it. In Cleveland were yet two more of Baba's half-sisters, Ruth and Anissa! Tempering the sense of coincidence just a bit, however, is the fact that the Great Lakes crescent from Cleveland to Detroit, with its then plentiful factory work, business opportunities, and preponderance of Little Syrias, was a magnet for Arab immigrants.

➤➤➤

In Damascus during my mother's childhood, cooking fuel was expensive, and only the rich could afford to bake their own bread. Every week neighborhood housewives would prepare their own bread dough and send it on trays to the corner baker, who charged them a small fee to bake it for them. It wasn't until these housewives, or their children, emigrated to America that they began to bake their own bread at home.

Saturday was baking day in our house, as it was at my cousin Mike's. The other day we were reminiscing over the phone about how it was on those Saturday mornings, awakening to the aromas of hot bread and the almost lemony sumac tang of za'atar, then later listening on the radio to *Sergeant Preston of the Yukon* as we lazily noshed on a breakfast of still-hot buttered bread.

A mixture of thyme, oregano, toasted sesame seeds, and sumac, za'atar is available at Middle eastern markets and online.

T'lamit Za'atar
(Thyme Loaves)

THE ZA'ATAR TOPPING:
¾ cup ground thyme
¼ cup sumac spice
3 tablespoons sesame seeds, toasted
½ teaspoon ground oregano
¼ teaspoon ground cinnamon
¼ teaspoon allspice
¼ teaspoon ground coriander
½ teaspoon salt

THE *TLAMEE* LOAVES:
4 cups all-purpose flour
1 teaspoon salt
1 packet dry yeast
1 teaspoon sugar
3 cups warm water, divided
½ cup olive oil, divided
4 tablespoons (½ stick) butter, melted

1. In a small bowl, combine all ingredients for za'atar topping and set aside.
2. Sift flour and salt into a large pan or mixing bowl. In a small bowl, dissolve yeast and sugar in ½ cup of the warm water.
3. Add yeast mixture to the flour, then add ¼ cup of the olive oil and remaining 2½ cups of warm water.
4. Mix together and knead until smooth and satiny.

5. Turn into greased bowl, cover, and set aside for 1 hour. (Or skip steps 2 through 4 and use store-bought pizza dough!)
6. Cut dough into 4 sections and shape sections into balls. Dust with flour, cover with plastic, and let sit for 30 minutes. Preheat oven to 475°F.
7. Pat or roll out each ball to ½-inch thickness. They can be round, like pizza, or oblong, the way my mother made them (probably to fit more on her baking sheet).
8. Combine remaining ¼ cup of the olive oil and the butter. Add enough of this mixture to the za'atar topping to form a thick paste. Brush each *talmiyeh* with za'atar topping.
9. Place on hot pizza stone or cookie sheet and bake until bottoms turn golden, and then put under broiler until tops are light brown.

➤ ➤ ➤

Pita Chips

3½ teaspoons za'atar topping
2 tablespoons extra-virgin olive oil
1 pocket pita

1. Preheat oven to 350°F. Stir together za'atar with oil to form a paste.
2. Separate pocket pita by slicing around the edge to create two rounds. Place rounds on a cookie sheet with inner or "rough" sides up.
3. Using a pastry brush, spread za'atar mix over surface of each round.
4. Bake until edges begin to crisp, 5 to 8 minutes. Let cool and slice into wedges.

About 12 to 18 chips. (Recipe can be doubled or tripled.)

➤ ➤ ➤

Serve Pita Chips with the following recipe, a yogurt-based chip dip.

Laban ou Toum
(Yogurt Chip Dip)

1 cup plain yogurt
Pinch of salt
1 tablespoon dried crushed mint
1 garlic clove, minced
1 tablespoon extra-virgin olive oil

Stir together all ingredients. Serve with pita chips.

➤ ➤ ➤

Batatat Za'atar
(Thyme Potatoes)

You'll find za'atar to be a quite versatile spice blend. Store it in a glass jar and keep handy. It's an essential ingredient in the Fattoush recipe (page 95) and delicious sprinkled on fried eggs or on potatoes.

1 pound potatoes (red or Yukon gold)
3 tablespoons extra-virgin olive oil
1 teaspoon salt
2 tablespoons za'atar
Zest of 1 lemon

1. Preheat oven to 400°F.
2. Boil the potatoes for about 10 to 12 minutes. Remove from pan, and when cool enough to handle, slice into rounds about ½-inch thick.
3. Toss sliced potatoes in a large bowl with olive oil, salt, and za'atar. Spread onto a cookie sheet.
4. Roast in the oven for 30 to 40 minutes. Remove. Sprinkle with lemon zest and serve.

Serves 2 to 3

Twelve

Il Amerkain

While Baba had been to America before, my mother was a total green-horn. She knew Arabic, of course, and some French, but not one word of English. In Syria she had led a sheltered life with very few modern conveniences. Which was why on one of her first forays into deepest America she found herself stopped dead in her tracks on the main floor of Tiedtke's Department Store. We, her three little children, stood close to her, facing a bewildering sight, a heavily crowded staircase. What baffled Mama was that something was different about this particular staircase, something she had heard of before but never actually seen—stairs that *moved*.

This is one of my earliest memories: Mama's hesitation just as she and my brother and sister and I all linked hands and stepped up to join the ascending file of people. I remember the crowd pressing from behind and, somehow, from *beneath* us too, as we tried to continue up the stairs. But the steps themselves were climbing faster than we were—even the banister was moving! It became dizzying! Suddenly, I lost Mama's hand. There was the crush of her heavy blue coat as she reached out and fell back onto me. The two of us tumbled backward into the crowd behind and below us. After us came my brother and sister, feet scrambling the air, still holding hands. There were shouts and screams and the rough grasp of strangers reaching out to catch hold of us. Other people started to go down. Finally, somebody somewhere threw a shut-off switch, and the escalator stopped moving.

Circled by a crowd of concerned Amerkain, Mama checked us kids for cuts or bruises and, finding none, dusted herself off and ushered us with great dignity through the parting crowd and out of the store. When Baba heard about all this he was furious, of course.

That's how he dealt with embarrassment. My mother was just the opposite. So warm and at home among family and the other *ibn Arab* of the neighborhood, Mama seemed to turn timidly stiff and formal among the Amerkain. Whenever she was among them, she did the simplest things in an exaggeratedly proper, even refined way, adjusting a napkin or gently blowing on a cup of hot coffee. It was as if she were being watched and saying to the Amerkain sitting around us at the Woolworth's lunch counter, "Do you see?"

➤ ➤ ➤

I began speaking English outside our family. I remember that it seemed easier to understand what the neighborhood kids were saying than it was to respond to them. I remember, too, how they mock-imitated my accent, and my lost, sinking feeling that my barely literate, Arabic-speaking family couldn't help me with this problem. We were each on our own, not only here among our neighborhood kids but in greater America as well. As I held my mother's gloved hand while she went shopping at the downtown department stores, at Tiedtke's or Lasalle's or the Lion Store, I worried about what I perceived as the impatience of the Amerkain, of bus drivers and clerks and the salesgirls who tapped a finger on the counter while they waited for her to make clear what she was asking for. I learned language so much faster than my mother that before long—accent or not—I was jumping in and translating for her.

Every time we returned home on the bus, I could sense her relief. It wasn't in Mama's nature to keep going out there and testing the American waters. Baba, hoping she might somehow absorb the language as if by osmosis, encouraged her to take us to the movies, to keep the radio on all day. For a while he even had her come downstairs and "help out" in the store.

Knowing French, Mama was able read the numbers on the cash register keys, and that is where Baba started her. The process must have looked odd to the Amerkain customers. Since Mama knew no English, Baba called out the prices in Arabic as he roamed the shelves with his grasping stick. She would translate the Arabic price into French, find the numbers on the cash register, and press the keys—*ka-ching!* As she handed the customer change, she dipped her chin and forced a smile. *Enwhaddyelse?* was the first English I ever heard my mother speak. But even such simple exchanges took a toll on her; fearing Baba's temper and assuming the customer's impatience, she would make mistakes, become frustrated. When that happened, Baba would nudge her aside and take over while she sat on the stool behind the counter and put her apron to her face.

➤➤➤

The kitchen in our flat above the store became Mama's refuge from this baffling new world she found herself in. She didn't know English and she didn't know the ways and means of America. She would learn most of these things, eventually, in her own good time. But for now, what she did know was how the food of her homeland was supposed to taste, and in that kitchen she began to learn how to create for her family those tastes of home. Her natural talent for cooking took her beyond Baba's teaching. One of her first masterpieces was Sheikh il Mihshee, or Lord of Stuffed Dishes.

Sheikh il Mihshee
(Stuffed Eggplant)

2 large eggplants
4 tablespoons (½ stick) butter, melted
1 pound lamb (or beef), coarsely ground
1 medium onion, diced small
½ teaspoon salt
¼ cup pine nuts
½ teaspoon black pepper
1 teaspoon ground cinnamon
½ teaspoon allspice
1 can (about 16 ounces) tomato sauce
Pinch of sugar
1½ cups water
¼ cup lemon juice
Riz bi Siriyeh (page 15)

1. Preheat oven to 450°F. Peel eggplants and cut lengthwise in wedges. Make a lengthwise slit in each wedge to form a long narrow pocket. (Take care not to cut through the bottoms!)
2. Arrange wedges in a baking dish, pocket-slit sides up, and brush them with butter. Bake for about 10 minutes, then remove from oven and let cool.

3. In a fry pan, brown the lamb with the onion and salt. Then stir in the pine nuts, pepper, cinnamon, and allspice. Continue to cook on medium heat for 3 to 4 minutes, then remove from heat and let cool.

4. Turn oven down to 350°F. Using a small spoon, or your fingers, fill each eggplant pocket with lamb stuffing. In a bowl, mix together the tomato sauce, sugar, and water. Carefully pour over the eggplants. Drizzle with the lemon juice. Bake for half an hour. Serve over Riz bi Siriyeh.

Serves 8

➤ ➤ ➤

Eggplant is one of those foods that tastes good hot or cold. For example, Lebanese Eggplant Cilantro Salad, a summertime favorite.

Salatet Beitenjain Kizberah
(Eggplant Cilantro Salad)

1 medium eggplant
1 tablespoon salt, or to taste
2 medium zucchini
2 tablespoons olive oil
¾ cup chopped fresh cilantro
¼ medium red onion, sliced thin
1 garlic clove, crushed
¼ red bell pepper, sliced thin
Juice of 1 lemon
Juice of ½ orange
½ teaspoon black pepper

1. Cut eggplant in half, lengthwise, then into ½-inch-thick half-moon slices. Place in a colander and sprinkle with salt. Let stand 30 minutes.

2. Meanwhile, peel zucchini, then slice thinly, either lengthwise with a potato peeler or crosswise with a mandoline, and set aside.

3. Rinse eggplant and pat dry. Brush both sides with olive oil and grill 3½ minutes per side, or until lightly browned. (Or cook under a broiler 3½ minutes to a side.) Set aside to cool.

4. Place eggplant, cilantro, red onion, garlic, zucchini, red bell pepper, lemon juice, orange juice, and black pepper in a bowl and toss to combine.

Serves 6

Thirteen

The Arda Muzeema

One of my earliest memories is of me in front of my father's store, fascinated at how Monroe Street's wide sidewalk kept spinning beneath my feet each time I looked down. My father's voice spoke my childhood name, "Zuzu." He came out of the store, the screen door clapping shut behind him. His apron was blinding white in the sunlight as he bent down and handed me a cold bottle of orange soda pop. Then he scooped me up and carried me out of the sun, setting me down in the shade of the store's front awning.

The two side-by-side doors of our entryway were open wide for air. The 902 door led into the store; next to it, the 902½ door opened onto the stairway leading up to our flat above the store. Mama sat at the top of the stairway, fanning herself with a piece of cardboard. "Look how the heat is making the children dizzy!" she called down, complaining. "There is no heat like this in the Old Country, not even in *djhennum il hamra!*" The very mention of the "red hell" was enough to signal fear in me, conjuring a desert wasteland where lurked the Arabic demons of my mother's cautionary stories, the *afareet* and the djinn. But at least the desert baked you quick. Unlike this muggy simmer that closed in on you, smothering and suffocating.

Toledo, originally named Frogtown, had been founded on a stretch of marshland, the Great Black Swamp, where the Maumee joined Lake Erie. During the dog days of summer, the air often turned boggy in this corner of northwest Ohio, and given the right combination of recent rainfall and air temperature inversion, it could stay like that for weeks. Electric fans helped, but not much. The only true respite came from air-conditioning, which in 1947 you had to go to "the show," or movies, to find.

"Go, take the children and go downtown to the show!" Baba suggested.

Mama continued fanning herself with a piece of newspaper. She was bored with going to the show. Twice this week she had taken us downtown on the bus to the Royal Theatre and to the Loop next door, to see Hopalong Cassidy, the Durango Kid, Lash LaRue, and—*aira condition* or no *aira condition*—she'd had enough of gunfire and bar room brawls and that maddening background noise to all of it, the incessant mooing of cattle. "Fine business!" She fanned harder.

Baba called to her up the stairway. "Then take them and go to the *arda muzeema!*"

Mama stopped fanning. "The what?"

Baba motioned her to come downstairs so they could talk *mittel naas*, that is, "like normal people," and not keep shouting up and down the stairwell.

Mama had a careful, sidestepping way of descending stairs, one tread at a time: left foot, right foot, pause, left foot, right foot, pause.

The *arda muzeema*, Baba explained, was a place where they had pictures on the walls. Fine statues. "They have gardens with benches to sit on and listen to fine music. And," he added, indicating the fan in Mama's hand, "they have the *aira condition*." Go, he urged her, *"Shimee il howah."* In English, "breathe the air." When people go for a Sunday drive in the country, or actually on any kind of brief outing, they go to *shim il howah*.

"How far is it, *il arda muzeema?*"

"Mish' safara," he explained, "not a long trek." The Toledo Art Museum was about a mile from the store, a straight shot up Monroe Street. We wouldn't even need to transfer buses.

"Well . . . ," Mama looked away and resumed fanning herself.

"Well, what?"

Well, she didn't like the idea of taking buses on her own. True, after almost a whole year in America, she knew which bus it was that takes her downtown and which brings her home again. But even on those familiar routes she feared the drivers might neglect to let her know when she'd reached her stop.

Baba shook his head slowly, a sign he was losing patience. He stepped to the cash register, wiped his hands across the stomach of his apron, opened the cash drawer, and took out several nickels. "Here. If you get lost, go to a telephone booth and call the store." Sighing with defeat, she slowly started back upstairs to pack a *zoueideh* for our journey into deepest America.

→→→

Zoueideh is the word for a Syrian take-along meal, and a homemaker traveled nowhere without a *zoueideh* because God forbid her family should be forced to stop at a restaurant and pay money to eat the food of strangers. We kids would be happy with peanut butter and jelly on white bread, but that wasn't what you'd find in a *zoueideh*. Cold food? Don't be silly. No, a proper *zoueideh* contained at least one actual cooked dish—tomato sauce and green beans on rice or lentils in caramelized onions, or maybe wrapped grape leaves or cabbage leaves. The cold food was for snacks only—*jibneh cheese* with olives wrapped in flatbread, pickled turnips and baby eggplants. Since neither purse nor lunch pail nor even Tupperware (had it existed then) could contain a proper *zoueideh*, you needed at least one double-handled shopping bag, and sometimes two.

According to the family story of that art museum visit, the *zoueideh* was the first thing to go wrong. As we lurched in our seats to the sudden stops and starts and swaying of the bus, we soon caught the aroma of the tomato garlic sauce, called *zoum*; the corner of the *zoueideh* bag was beginning to darken. The thermos bottle Mama used to keep the *zoum* warm had begun to leak. Luckily, it was only a couple stops later that the driver turned to tell us we'd reached the art museum. We stepped down, my brother, my sister, and I, then Mama, the *zoum* dripping from the bottom of her *zoueideh* bag. The sidewalk was burning hot, even in the shade, as we watched the bus rumble away in its wheeze of diesel smoke.

But after it had passed, we saw no *arda muzeema*. Only wide expanses of fresh-clipped lawns. There were signs everywhere, but we couldn't read them, and we weren't even sure what exactly it was we were looking for anyway. A building with pictures on the walls? With music? With benches and air-conditioning?

My brother, Aboody, heard the music first, strains of it from just around the corner. The four of us set off following the sound, while the dripping *zoueideh* left a trail of *zoum* spatters behind us. Rounding the corner, we came upon a small glassed-in building in the center of a freshly tarred parking lot. The music was coming from loudspeakers on the roof. The front of the little building had large plateglass windows that had been brightly painted with cartoon characters, some of which we gleefully recognized from the movies: Porky Pig, Woody Woodpecker, Tweety Bird. There were red and white pennants strung from the roof out to a large sign pole that bore at its summit the circular painting of a flying red horse with wings. A voice on the loudspeaker announced a grand opening. We'd found it—the *arda muzeema*! The only things missing were benches on the narrow strip of grass that bordered the parking lot. Mama shook her head. No air-conditioning, either. She unfolded a large cloth napkin from the *zoueideh* and spread it out. She motioned us to sit down on the grass around it. She began taking food out, and we ate, fanning ourselves with waxed paper. It took our minds off the heat to watch how busy the place was, how cars kept driving up to the little building and men in crisp new uniforms hurried about filling them with gas, wiping windshields, and checking tires.

Then one car pulled out of the customer line and stopped short. Its door swung open and we saw, stepping out to wave us over, Charlotte and Danny Bertman, our Amerkain neighbors from around the corner. Danny opened the back door of his sedan. "Get in!" he urged us, smiling and shaking his head. "C'mon, get in!"

➤ ➤ ➤

In almost every *zoueideh* you'll find a wonderfully portable snack, rolled grape leaves, or *warak enib*. Grape leaves in jars of a hundred or so can be found in most supermarkets (usually near the olives). Or you can pick your own. Wild grape leaves will be more tender than most store-bought. Jarred grape leaves need to be rinsed of brine before use. But to prepare fresh leaves, you need only dip each leaf for a second or two in simmering hot water, then set it to blot on paper towels. When dry, the softened leaves can be used right away for rolling or be packed together in plastic bags and frozen to be used later. I like to decorate a platter of tabouli (page 41) with lemon-soaked grape leaves, using the smaller, more tender leaves for scooping or pinching the tabouli into a *litmeh* (morsel), which I pop into my mouth.

In the Midwest, grape leaves can be found all summer long, but the best time for picking would be the young leaves of late May and early June. Many a Sunday drive to visit Aunt Yemnah in Bryan, Ohio, was interrupted by my mother noticing a cluster of wild grapevines in some field along the way. Dad would pull over, out would come the grocery sacks, and off my mother would send my brother and sister and me into the field to *howish*, or "pick," grape leaves. The best place to *howish* in the city itself was—and might still be—on Collingwood Boulevard, along the south brick wall of the Glaza Barber Shop across the parking lot from Coyle's mortuary.

Warak Enib Mihshee
(Stuffed Grape Leaves)

75 to 100 grape leaves, stems pinched off

THE FILLING:
1 cup uncooked short-grained rice
1 pound ground lamb
1 tablespoon ground cinnamon
1 teaspoon allspice
2 teaspoons salt
½ teaspoon black pepper
1 tablespoon olive oil
1 egg, beaten
Optional additions to the filling: pine nuts, dried mint, and finely chopped
   onion or shallots

FOR THE COOKING:
1 tablespoon olive oil
2 tablespoons butter, melted
1 large potato, cut in ¼-inch slices
4 to 5 garlic cloves, sliced
4 to 5 Greek olives (optional)
1 tablespoon beef base or bullion in 2 cups water for a broth
Juice of 2 lemons (approximately 5 to 6 tablespoons)

TO PREPARE THE FILLING:
1. Soak rice in lukewarm water to cover; after 20 minutes, drain.
2. Wet hands with cold water and hand mix rice with remaining filling
    ingredients in a large bowl.

TO STUFF THE LEAVES:
3. If using store-bought grape leaves, rinse in cold water and drain; before
    rolling, pour boiling water to cover, then drain. If using fresh-picked, wash
    grape leaves in hot tap water, drain, let dry on paper towels. (For use at
    a later time, pack in plastic bags and freeze. This keeps the color bright;
    after thawing about 5 minutes in cold water, they will be limp enough to
    roll.) Go through grape leaves and separate out and set aside a few large,
    already torn ones.
4. Take one grape leaf at a time, place on towel with veiny side up toward
    you. Place 1 to 1½ teaspoons of filling on the wide bottom, about ¼
    inch from the stem; form filling into a log shape. (Don't overstuff, or the
    expanding rice will burst the leaves!) Fold up from the bottom once and
    stop, fold the left and right sides in toward the middle, then continue

rolling up and away from you. Set the stuffed grape leaf aside with the fold seam on the bottom.

TO COOK:

1. Swirl olive oil and butter around the bottom of a Dutch oven. In order to prevent sticking, line bottom with potato slices, and then the large, torn grape leaves.
2. Arrange the rolled grape leaves in rows along the bottom. Alternating the direction of each layer, top each layer with garlic slices. Toss in the Greek olives if using.
3. Press grape leaves down with an inverted dish; place a bowl filled with water (for weight) atop the dish. Add enough broth to the rolled grape leaves to cover the inverted dish.
4. Bring to boil. Adjust heat to a slow-bubble boil; after 15 minutes, add the lemon juice. Another 10 minutes and they're done!

Serve hot with lemon wedge and a dab of ice-cold yogurt or *labneh* (similar to Greek yogurt, this is plain yogurt that develops a thickened tanginess after being strained a day or so in a cheesecloth hung from the kitchen faucet).

Tips: For a richer broth, add lamb bones to the bottom of the pot, along with the potato slices. Lemon slices between the layers of rolled leaves contribute tang and brightness, as would a stalk or two of rhubarb.

➻ ➻ ➻

Zoueideh food is, of course, also picnic food. And the two salad recipes below are picnic standards.

Summers in Toledo, the families used to gather for huge joint picnics at the North End's Riverside Park, or in later years, to the south at Walbridge Park. On the Fourth of July, one of the old-timers would be helped up onto a picnic table to give a patriotic speech. Because it was delivered in High Arabic, it was an oration that only a few of the listeners understood anymore. With its almost poetic intonations and repetitions, High Arabic was probably as far across the language spectrum as a person could get from Kitchen Arabic, which was fast becoming the only Arabic the younger generations understood anymore. We all knew the speech was patriotic, though, because every so often we heard the word "America" pop up in the midst of an emotional rush of unintelligible, highfalutin verbiage, and the speaker would pause briefly, bow his head, and put a hand over his heart.

➻ ➻ ➻

Salata Batata
(Lebanese Potato Salad)

3 pounds potatoes (red skin, russet, Yukon gold, or a combination)
1 onion
¼ cup olive oil
1 bunch scallions, chopped
1 small garlic clove
1 teaspoon kosher salt
½ cup lemon juice
¼ teaspoon black pepper
¼ cup chopped mint (or 2 tablespoons dried mint)
½ cup chopped parsley

1. Boil potatoes, with the onion, till fork tender. Discard onion and let potatoes cool; then peel, cube, and transfer potatoes to a large salad bowl.
2. Add oil and stir, coating potatoes. Add scallions and mix well.
3. Smash garlic onto salt, pressing to create a paste. Transfer to a small bowl. Stir in the lemon juice, pepper, and mint. Pour contents over potatoes and stir to mix in.
4. Place in the fridge for a couple hours at least to chill and let flavors develop.
5. Top with parsley and serve.

Serves 6

➤➤➤

In Damascus, during prolonged heat waves, according to Mama, the earth would sometimes tremble. Even years afterward, safe in rock-solid Toledo, she still felt the old dread, especially amid the dog days of August when the weather got hot and still.

What follows is her go-to cold soup recipe for summer evenings during "Earthquake Season" . . . a cooling concoction of cucumber and yogurt, lemon and mint.

Shorabet Khiyar bi Laban
(Cold Cucumber-Yogurt Soup)

2½ cups plain yogurt
½ cup sour cream
2 tablespoons extra-virgin olive oil
2 cups cucumber, seeded and diced, julienned, grated,
    or thinly sliced on a mandolin
1 cup milk
½ to 1 cup fresh dill, chopped
¼ cup scallions, chopped
¼ cup fresh mint, chopped
1 tablespoon dried mint, crushed
½ teaspoon salt
1 teaspoon white pepper
2 tablespoons lemon juice

1. Whisk together yogurt, sour cream, and olive oil until smooth. Stir in cucumber.
2. Add milk, dill, scallions, fresh mint, dried mint, salt, white pepper, and lemon juice.
3. Stir, cover, and refrigerate until well chilled.

Serves 6 to 8

Note: Garnish each serving with a sprinkle of chopped chives and a thin sliver or two of red bell pepper. Serve with 1 ramekin of golden raisins and 1 of walnuts or toasted pine nuts, to pass.

Fourteen

Charlotte and Danny

We had no yard on Monroe Street, no neighborhood playground, so like most city kids, we played on the streets and in vacant lots. One day when I was chasing after my brother and sister down the gravel stone alleyway behind the store, I was startled by the vivid sensation of my shoe thumping against something turgid and thick. Stopping short, I turned to look: a dead rat. A fat one. Poison was used to control them, and they died wherever the poison finished its work—in walls, behind refrigerators, or right out in the middle of the open alleyway. This being primarily a business district, all the alley doors as well as most of the street-side doors had their lower sections sheathed in galvanized metal.

There were other dangers in our neighborhood, as well. My brother, Aboody, tells the story of a close call I'd had as a toddler. Only a little over a year older than me, Aboody was "watching" me as we played on the crowded sidewalk in front of the Monroe Bar right next door to Baba's store. I was too young to remember any of this, of course, but apparently a drunken stranger stepped out of the bar, casually reached down, gripped my hand, and began walking off with me. Alarmed, Aboody began to wail, so loudly and with such sudden intensity that the driver of a bus idling nearby climbed down to see what was the trouble. Aboody pointed to the drunk, stumbling and weaving as he continued walking me away. "That bum," he sobbed, "he took my brother!" Immediately, the driver pulled a blackjack from his hip pocket, ran up behind the stranger, and sapped him a good one. The drunk let go my hand, and the bus driver led me back to my brother.

So, where were our parents during all this? Neighbors always watched out for neighborhood kids back in the Old Country, and I think Mama and Baba must have assumed the same applied to Monroe Street.

One of our neighbors, Charlotte Bertman, ran the office of her husband Danny's auto trim business at Tenth and Jefferson, just around the block from us. As a group of us kids paraded by that corner, I remember her at the shop window, smiling at us from her desk. Charlotte was probably in her early forties when we met her, and for reasons never explained to us kids, she couldn't have children, although she very much wanted to. Which was probably why she took such a shine to us, and especially to Aboody. A jabbery five-year-old, he had a head of thick curls and a spunky attitude. Charlotte and Danny sometimes stopped by our store on weekends with a treat or some trinket they'd picked up shopping. I remember them taking my brother and me for outings to the Toledo Zoo, downtown for the Saturday movie serials, and even to the art museum (the real one!). Like the rest of us, Mama grew fond of Charlotte and Danny—so generous, so kind and sweet natured, what's not to like?—but at the beginning she had been leery of them because they were, after all, Jewish. Growing up in Damascus, Mama had been steeped in all the old prejudices. Her family, largely unschooled, had never been educated beyond cultural traditions and superstitions; to them the evil eye was a real thing. As was anything the local priests told them, no matter how off the wall; one priest in particular, Mama's uncle Alexios, told stories about how Christ-killing Jews kidnapped Christian children and drank their blood in secret ceremonies. One of the oldest, and most malicious, of conspiracy theories.

(And you don't have to go all the way to the Middle East to find such ugly stories, either; in the 1920s and 1930s, Henry Ford was publishing the exact same libels in his Dearborn, Michigan, newspapers.)

So, given her background, how had Mama overcome such prejudice? I think the answer is there in that background. Because her people had little to no schooling, they had to trust experience, common sense, and good-heartedness. And her people possessed great courage: during the Ottoman genocide of the Armenians, Mama's family had risked their home and their very lives to protect an Armenian woman and her daughter, hiding the two of them away in the cellar for nearly a year until it was safe again to surface. Thus, in the very childhood home where my mother had learned prejudice, she'd also learned to trust compassion, a quality that trumps prejudice. In short, Mama got to know Charlotte and Danny.

Our family knew them for too short a time. After four years we moved from that apartment above the Monroe Street store. Not long after, we learned that Danny had passed away. Charlotte followed him only a few years after, when I was around twelve. The last time I saw her was on a Christmas Eve, when, a lonely widow, she joined us for Midnight Mass at the cathedral. Since she wasn't Christian, I was surprised that she loved and sang along to the carols.

➤ ➤ ➤

My wife, Fern, also Jewish, also loves Christmas carols. Born in the Bronx, she learned to sing all of the beautiful ones—from "O Holy Night" to "What Child Is This?"—in her elementary school, PS 95, which had over 90 percent Jewish students.

To the memory of Charlotte and Danny, and to celebrate the enjoyment of new things from different cultures, here are some recipes that I learned to make from my wife's side of the family.

➤ ➤ ➤

Fern's Aunt Gertie's Noodle Kugel

12-ounce package wide egg noodles
6 eggs, beaten
2 cups small curd cottage cheese
2 cups sour cream
1 ½ cups white sugar, divided
6 tablespoons (¾ stick) butter, melted
1 tablespoon vanilla extract
1 teaspoon salt
½ cup raisins (optional)
¼ cup brown sugar
1 teaspoon ground cinnamon

1. Preheat oven to 375°F; spray or grease a 9-by-13-inch baking dish.
2. Bring large pot of salted water to boil, add egg noodles, stirring occasionally, till firm but cooked through (approximately 5 minutes).
3. Meanwhile, mix together eggs, cottage cheese, sour cream, 1 cup of the white sugar, butter, vanilla extract, salt, and raisins (if using) in a large bowl.
4. Drain egg noodles and stir them into the mixture, then pour mixture into the baking dish.
5. Combine the remaining ½ cup of the white sugar with the brown sugar and cinnamon in a small bowl; sprinkle this mixture atop the noodle kugel.

6. Bake until bubbly and the noodles are golden (approximately 1 hour). Allow kugel to cool on a wire rack about 10 minutes before serving.

Serves 8 to 12

➤➤➤

Potato Kugel

As a potato side dish, this savory version of the kugel has become a family favorite.

6 eggs
½ cup oil
4 tablespoons all-purpose flour
1 tablespoon salt
1 teaspoon black pepper
8 medium potatoes
2 onions, quartered
2 to 3 average-sized carrots, peeled (optional)

1. Preheat the oven to 400°F.
2. In a large bowl, mix the eggs, oil, flour, and salt and pepper. Set the bowl aside while you work on the vegetables.
3. Set up a food processor to use the coarse grating disk (large holes). Peel and rinse the potatoes under running water, and then begin feeding them into food processor. (You may need to cut them to fit in the mouth of the machine.)
   Coarsely grate all of the potatoes. Place them into a colander, and put the colander into the sink. Let stand for 3 to 5 minutes.
4. Cut onions so they fit into the food processor and grate them in the food processor. Then grate the carrots, if using. (Carrots are optional, but I learned to add them for color and a hint of sweetness.)
5. Grease a 9-by-13-inch baking dish.
6. A handful at a time, squeeze out the excess liquid from the potatoes.
7. In a large bowl, mix together the potatoes, onions, and carrots. Then add and stir in the egg mixture.
8. Pour the mixture into the baking dish.
9. Bake uncovered for 1 hour or until the top is golden brown. When you insert a knife in the middle, it should come out clean. Enjoy!

➤➤➤

Fern's friend Debbie makes the best Hanukkah brisket ever, and using one of the simplest recipes, which she graciously shared with me.

Debbie's Aunt Helen's Brisket

4-to-6-pound brisket
1 to 2 packets of onion soup mix
Seasonings of your choice, such as garlic powder, fresh rosemary, and black pepper—salt is not necessary as soup mix has plenty
1 bouillon cube, crumbled, or 1 teaspoon beef base, such as Better Than Bouillon
1 bottle (750 ml) of hearty red wine
½ cup water

1. Preheat oven to 300°F.
2. Line a roasting pan with heavy-duty aluminum foil. Sprinkle with onion soup mix, then add brisket, seasonings, bouillon, wine, and water.
3. Fold foil tightly around the brisket so that it does not leak.
4. Bake in oven for 5 hours.
5. Slice brisket and replace slices in the juice. Keep warm or refrigerate and reheat tomorrow. It is always better the next day!

➜ ➜ ➜

Matzo brei is a kind of comfort-food dish that features the simple, homey flavors called *haimish* in Yiddish. I learned the following easy-to-prepare version from Fern's mom, Ruth.

Grandma Ruth's Basic Matzo Brei

4 matzo crackers
4 eggs
Salt and black pepper, to taste
1 tablespoon butter

OPTIONAL VARIATIONS:
½ small onion, grated
1 teaspoon vanilla
½ teaspoon ground cinnamon

1. Break matzo crackers into small pieces into a small bowl.
2. Cover with hot tap water for a minute, then use your hands to squeeze out the water.
3. In a medium bowl, beat eggs with salt and pepper, and add the matzo. Mix well. To try a variation on the standard, stir in any of the optional ingredients or any combination of them.
4. Heat a medium size fry pan, add butter. Pour the matzo-egg mixture into frypan. Brown on one side and turn over. Let cook about 1 minute, then serve.

Serve with jam or maple syrup.

Serves 4

Fifteen

A Setup

It was a snowy weekday afternoon, and I was about four years old. With my brother and sister away at school, I often spent hours sprawled on the floor, drawing with crayons on lengths of butcher paper from my father's store downstairs. As I finished each picture, I proudly presented it to my mother. On this day, one drawing in particular caught her interest. "*Shu ha'ad?*" she asked, "What is this?" as she pointed to my rendering of a little boy.

"*Annah*," I tell her, "It's me." The boy was standing akimbo, legs apart, hands on his hips.

She smiled, then moved her finger to a wide, roughly circular shape in front of the figure. "And this?"

"That's our toilet." (In Arabic, *sishmeh*.)

"So this is your pee?" she asked, indicating the crayoned arc streaming into the *sishmeh*.

"Yes!" I remember being pleased that she could so easily make out what I intended. The fact that I'd drawn something and she could actually make out what it was? Why, it was almost like writing, a skill my sister, VeeVee, three years my senior, was only beginning to learn!

Then Mama pointed again, her fingertip tracing the yellow arc back to its source. "And this?"

The answer was obvious. I shrugged. "That's my *menneh*!" I said, using the baby word for "penis." As soon as the word was out of my mouth, the drawing dropped from her hand, and she slapped me.

Oh, the shock of it! I'd been set up, and by my own mother!

By all rights I should have stopped drawing right there—but I didn't. And I don't remember harboring any hard feelings, either. My mother loved me, I knew that. Almost as important, I knew that I was innocent of any bad intent. And I could tell that *she* knew that the drawing was one of my good ones. In fact, I remember feeling a kind of pride that I didn't have words for yet: I had actually drawn something that had evinced an emotional reaction. The very essence of art!

>->->

After thirty-five years of teaching, I took the leap and retired from the Iowa State University English Department. Shortly afterward, I bought an easel at an estate sale. The thing looked huge to me, but the price was right—they were practically giving it away—so what the heck. I took it home and stored it away in my basement. All my life I'd been drawing and doodling; as an undergraduate in college I even completed a couple oils. Now that I was retired, maybe someday I might give painting another go.

That "someday" wouldn't dawn until that easel had sat in my basement for nearly a full ten years. The cliché about retirement being busier than working life proved all too true for me. I overcommitted myself to a flurry of busyness: community volunteering, writing, editing, publishing, giving cooking classes. But eventually I was able to ease up, and there came a quiet stretch where I found myself with time on my hands. What to do?

Well, I did have this easel downstairs that I'd stowed away a decade ago.

Our house has a finished basement, featuring a large room with a fireplace, where I have my writing desk and a poker table; a smaller room just off it was once a kitchen, with a fridge and a sink in one corner. In the opposite corner, right next to a large window well, is the perfect spot for setting up an easel. Why not? Out shopping I went and brought home brushes, acrylic paints, a couple prestretched canvases, and I got busy again.

>->->

One of the activities that kept me busy in retirement was teaching cooking classes, where I introduced my Iowa audiences to Middle Eastern fare. One of their favorites was the following eggplant recipe, which they enjoyed almost as much for its name as for its wonderful flavors. Imam Beyildi translates to "the imam fainted." The reasons differ about why the imam (a Muslim prayer leader) fainted. One interpretation says it's because the flavor is so dizzyingly wonderful, while another version has him fainting when he learns that his wife used up all the olive oil in the house to make it. The recipe below can be eaten hot or cold. As for me, I go with the Syrian old-wives' admonishment that no olive oil dish should be eaten hot lest it make you light-headed!

Imam Beyildi
(The Imam Fainted)

¾ cup olive oil, divided
2 medium onions, chopped
2 garlic cloves, minced
½ cup chopped fresh parsley (or cilantro)
2 tablespoons chopped basil
2 tablespoons chopped dill
1 can (28 ounces) diced tomatoes
1 tablespoon dried mint
1 teaspoon salt
½ teaspoon black pepper
2 medium eggplants, stem ends cut off
2 teaspoons sugar
¼ cup lemon juice

1. In a large skillet bring ¼ cup of the olive oil to a shimmer over medium heat and sauté the onions until they begin to soften, about 3 to 5 minutes.
2. Stir in garlic, parsley, basil, dill, and tomatoes, and cook until ingredients thicken and liquid is mostly reduced. Stir in the mint, salt, and pepper. Remove from heat and set aside to cool.
3. Cut eggplants in half lengthwise. Make 2 lengthwise slits (about 1 inch deep) in the flesh to within a half inch of each end.
4. In a large skillet, heat the remaining ½ cup of the olive oil to a shimmer over medium-high heat and fry the eggplant, cut side down, until the flesh is dark gold in color.
5. Turn the eggplants over and fry on the skin side, 2 to 3 minutes more, then remove from pan (reserving the oil), and place eggplants on paper towels to drain and cool, about 20 minutes.
6. Preheat oven to 325°F. Place eggplants skin side down in a 9-by-13-inch baking dish. Open a gap in each slit and fill with tomato mixture. Spoon any extra filling around the eggplants.
7. Sprinkle sugar over the eggplants, then drizzle on the lemon juice and the reserved olive oil.
8. Bake about 1¼ hours. Eggplants will collapse and flatten a bit. That's good.
9. Serve hot over rice, or at room temperature with a nice bread.

Serves 4

Sixteen

Bookra Mishmish

Down the block from my father's grocery on Monroe Street was a four-chair barber shop, where men in suits and wide-brimmed fedoras used to stop by for a shave and shoeshine as part of their daily routines. One in particular, Dr. Emidio Gaspari, had his office just around the corner in the Medical Arts Building.

It was through the barber shop that Dad got to know Dr. Gaspari, and the two of them hit it off from the start. The doctor, being Italian, resembled my *ibn Arab* "uncles"—dark haired, deep chested, and in late middle age, tending to thickness in the middle. Your run-of-the-mill Mediterranean immigrant male . . . until he opened his mouth to speak. Dr. Gaspari's voice was beyond loud, it was downright stentorian. In his office, he spoke directly, at times jokingly, but always with kindness. That was him: blunt, warmhearted, and loud. Very loud. Not shouting or yelling. I mean his voice simply *carried*; it traveled through walls, through the waiting room, and into the hallway. People in the Medical Arts Building, which was on Michigan Avenue just around the corner from our store, used to joke that you could hear Dr. Gaspari while you were still in the elevator.

Once, I sat in his waiting room, listening along with everybody else, while Dr. Gaspari examined my father.

"What's the trouble today, Geha?"

Baba said something, but through the closed door I could make out not a single word, only the familiar but muffled murmur of his voice. For weeks now he had been complaining of an achy discomfort in his leg, and I knew he wanted something for the pain.

The doctor's reply came through clear as a bell. "Geha, you're born with pain, you live with pain, you're gonna die with pain. All right, sit up here, let's have a look."

Whenever my mother took me along with her to his office, she often brought Dr. Gaspari a dish of whatever she'd cooked for supper the night before. He loved her cooking, especially the lamb-with-yogurt dishes, like *laban ommu*. As I sat in the waiting room, I could hear Dr. Gaspari ask her sarcastically, "Carmen, how's that husband of yours? You still living with that son of a bitch?" Mom laughed. Dr. Gaspari laughed. And everybody next door in the waiting room laughed.

"Geha," he said to me many times as I sat with my feet dangling from the edge of the examining table, "when you came to this country you were fulla worms and I had to clean you out!" Afterward, making a beeline for the door, I could hear suppressed tittering as I crossed the waiting room.

Dr. Gaspari died of a heart attack while I was still in my teens. My last memory of him is from one of the last times he saw me as a patient. Earlier, he'd inoculated me for smallpox, and I'd come back so he could check on how the inoculation was progressing. "Geha, take off your shirt." Sitting on his wheeled stool, he took a careful look at my upper arm, at the hot red scab that was forming. "Beautiful," he bellowed, then scooted back on the stool and, smiling benignly, thrust both arms out wide. "Blooming like a rose!" he announced to me, to everyone in the waiting room, to the entire floor of the Michigan Avenue Medical Arts Building.

To this day, I remember that moment as a kind of benediction: *Go forth and thrive!*

➜➜➜

Dr. Gaspari loved lamb dishes sauced with yogurt, like this "Lamb Supreme."

Laban Ommu
(Stew of Lamb in Yogurt Sauce)

7 to 8 small whole onions, peeled
4 tablespoons (½ stick) butter, divided
2 tablespoons olive oil
1½ pounds lamb shoulder or leg, in 1½-inch cubes
1 teaspoon ground cinnamon
½ teaspoon allspice

2 teaspoons salt, divided
½ teaspoon black pepper
2 cups chicken broth
1 quart plain yogurt
2 to 3 garlic cloves, mashed
1 tablespoon arrowroot dissolved in 2 tablespoons water
1 egg, well beaten
2 tablespoons dried mint
⅓ cup toasted pine nuts
2 tablespoons chopped fresh mint (or parsley)

1. In a Dutch oven, sauté onions in 1 tablespoon of the butter and the 2 tablespoons of the olive oil until nicely browned. Remove with slotted spoon and set aside.
2. Using the same pan and oil, brown the meat. Sprinkle in cinnamon, allspice, 1 teaspoon of the salt, and the pepper. Add broth and bring to a boil. Lower heat to simmer, cover Dutch oven, and continue to simmer for about 1½ hours.
3. In a medium bowl, mix together yogurt, the remaining 1 teaspoon of the salt, garlic, dissolved arrowroot, egg, and dried mint. Stir well and pour over meat in Dutch oven, add the onions, and let cook 20 minutes.
4. Serve over Riz bi Siriyeh (page 15). Sprinkle with toasted pine nuts and chopped fresh mint or parsley.

Serves 6 to 8

➤ ➤ ➤

Back in our Monroe Street days, Toledo didn't have any specialty groceries like you find today. Lebanese cooks had to bake their own flat bread, culture their own *laban* and *jibneh* cheese, grow their own *koosa* squash, pick their own grape leaves, and brew their own arak. But for the host of other ingredients that couldn't be made at home, they relied on weekly visits from the man from Detroit known familiarly as "the Armenian." Every Saturday he drove down to Toledo in his red panel truck. Parking in an empty lot in the North End, he would put on a white butcher's coat, raise a side panel on his truck, and reveal to the housewives of Little Syria the various goods imported all the way from the Old Country, via Detroit: the Armenian had bulghur, essential for kibbeh and tabouli, and he had *kishik*, too, along with tahini and pomegranate molasses and orange-blossom water, briny olives and dried *ful* beans.

One item I remember in particular was *amardeen*, a kind of candied pressed fruit leather made of dried apricots rolled flat. It had a bright fruit flavor and it was very sweet, so of course we kids loved it. The fact that it came from Damascus, Mama's hometown, somehow made it even more special. Unlike the fruit rollups that would become popular many decades later, *amardeen* came folded into thick, one-pound packages wrapped in yellow cellophane that you had to peel back to get at all that condensed flavor.

The deep yellow of the cellophane fascinated us. My brother and sister and I used to peel away wide strips of cellophane and hold them to our eyes, amazed at how the whole world changed in a blink, and the grayest Toledo day was made to look as bright and sunlit as memories of the Old Country.

➤➤➤

There's a saying I heard growing up, *bookra mishmish*, which translates literally to "tomorrow the apricots." Kind of an ancient Arabic version of "*mañana*" or "don't worry, be happy," it's used to allay concerns for the future. We won't go hungry, the saying assures us, because soon the apricots will be ripe!

Below is a recipe based on apricots that's possibly as old as *bookra mishmish*: the earliest known version of it appeared in *Katib al-Tabikh*, a cookbook written in Bagdad by Muḥammad bin al-Ḥasan bin Muḥammad bin al-Karīm al-Baghdadi in 1226.

Mishmishiyeh
(Lamb with Apricots)

1 cup dried apricots
½ cup sherry wine (or broth), heated
½ cup honey
¼ cup white vinegar
1 tablespoon Worcestershire sauce
1 tablespoon crushed red pepper flakes
2 garlic cloves, crushed
1 teaspoon ground coriander
1 teaspoon ground cumin
½ teaspoon ground turmeric

½ teaspoon ground cinnamon
½ teaspoon grated ginger root
Salt and black pepper
2 pounds lamb (shoulder or leg, trimmed, in ½-inch cubes)
2 to 3 tablespoons olive oil
1 medium onion, thinly sliced
¼ cup slivered almonds
½ yellow (or red) bell pepper, sliced into sticks
1½ cups chicken stock
Prepared couscous (see below)
1 package (10 ounces) washed arugula
Dollop or 2 of dark molasses
Rose (or orange-blossom) water
¼ cup chopped fresh cilantro and/or parsley

1. In a small bowl, soak the apricots in the sherry.
2. Make the spice sauce in a medium bowl by stirring together the honey, vinegar, Worcestershire, red pepper flakes, garlic, coriander, cumin, turmeric, cinnamon, and ginger.
3. Salt and pepper the lamb, and using a Dutch oven or large pan, such as a chicken fryer, brown the meat in the olive oil over medium-high heat. Remove the lamb, place it in the bowl with the spice sauce, toss to coat, and set aside.
4. In the same oil (adding a bit more, if needed), sauté the onion using medium heat, approximately 4 to 5 minutes, then add the slivered almonds. Stir, wait a minute or so, and add the yellow bell pepper sticks.
5. Slowly add chicken stock (to cover, up to 1½ cups), stirring to bring up the bits that have caramelized to the bottom. Add the lamb and spice sauce. Bring mixture to a simmer, about 20 minutes.
6. Make couscous (see below). Spoon couscous onto a bed of arugula.
7. Raise heat to reduce liquid, stirring in the molasses to help this process along.
8. Ladle contents of pan onto the couscous. Sprinkle with rose water and cilantro and/or parsley.

Serves 6 to 8

THE COUSCOUS:
1 tablespoon olive oil
½ teaspoon salt
½ teaspoon ground cumin
1 teaspoon ground coriander
1 teaspoon ground cardamom
¼ teaspoon cayenne pepper
½ teaspoon allspice
1 cup chicken broth
1 cup orange juice
1 tablespoon dried mint
¼ cup golden raisins
1½ cups couscous

1. In a medium saucepan heat oil to a shimmer, add salt, cumin, coriander, cardamom, cayenne, and allspice. Stir a minute to bring out aroma.
2. Pour in broth and orange juice, stir in mint, bring to a boil.
3. Add raisins and couscous, stir, cover, and remove from heat.
4. After 5 minutes, fluff with a fork and serve.

Seventeen

The Pigeonman

Ali Dahr's Monroe Street Bar used to be on the corner of Monroe Street and Michigan Avenue, right next door to my father's store. There were two other bars on that same corner, and a fourth just a couple doors up from us. These places weren't ye olde taverns or neighborhood pubs but hard-drinking saloons, open for business six days a week. Back then everyone I knew referred to the clientele of these establishments as "bums," or in Kitchen Arabic, *il bumiyeh*. On Sundays they would come into my father's grocery (open seven days a week) for pint bottles of wine—white port, Tokay, muscatel—which Baba sold under the counter, wrapped in butcher paper.

There weren't any parks or even much green space in our near-downtown area. Monroe Street's wide sidewalks extended from curb to doorstep, and during the warm weather months the *bumiyeh* filled those sidewalks, weaving and tottering their way from bar to bar or simply loitering, one foot propped behind them against the warm brick. Seemingly lethargic, they were capable of startling alacrity as they dashed to scoop up a tossed-away cigarette or cigar butt. They were almost all men, but I remember there were women *bumiyeh*, too. One in particular used to dress in trousers and jacket like a man and was nicknamed "Mona Lisa" after a song that was popular on the radio back then. Back then being the mid- to late 1940s, many of the *bumiyeh* were recent veterans, and many had a lot of fight still in them. Alcohol-fueled street brawls would erupt without warning.

The day I turned five, I remember horsey-hopping down our front stairs in my new birthday cowboy hat and singing to myself, "I'm cowboy Joe!" I horsey-hopped right out the front door of 902½ and almost smack into a loose circle of *bumiyeh*. A strange noise stopped me, made me look up. It was a hollow sound, like a watermelon knock, only much louder. As I stood frozen, a blood-flecked strand of spittle flew past me and slapped wetly against the doorpost next to my face. Then somebody spun me around and pushed me back inside the doorway. Even so, I'd seen enough so that I would ever after retain a perfectly clear image of two bums standing their ground and knocking their fists hard and loud against the sides of each other's heads.

➤ ➤ ➤

But most of the *bumiyeh* weren't violent or dangerous, and occasionally Dad would even hire one or another of them to haul away trash or do other odd jobs. There was Old Bill, a man in his seventies who swept the back room and fashioned hats for us kids out of newspaper; and Danny, who had three fingers missing on one hand and a way of imitating cartoon voices that kept us in hysterics. Another of the *bumiyeh* was a tall, very thin man who kept his distance from us kids, and we knew him only by his nickname, "the Pigeonman." In the quiet of an early summer morning, he could be seen stalking the sidewalks, fishing rod at the ready. The rod had an oversized reel on it, and dangling several inches from the tip was a heavy sinker; above that a puff of snelled fishhooks danced and sparkled in the sunlight. As he walked he kept his eyes raised, scanning the ledges and ornate cornices that adorned the upper stories of the old brick buildings. When he caught sight of what he was after, he stopped short, released about a foot of line, and began slowly swinging the tip of the fishing rod in wider and wider arcs, gaining momentum. Then, faster than I could follow, he'd already cast, and the line was whirring out and up, up until there was a thump as the sinker hit and the hooks took hold. The struck pigeon dropped, flapping against the line, while a flock of its brothers and sisters and cousins burst into the air. Their wings made a distant noise that to me was like the sound of applause fading on the radio.

Later, the Pigeonman brought his morning's catch around the alley to the back door of my father's store. If one of the birds looked seriously injured, Baba simply twisted its neck—one wing slowly stretching out, then a quick, cellophanelike crackle. Uninjured birds he placed in a bread deliveryman's box on the floor of the back room. Topped with a length of chicken wire, the box was deep with rounded corners and a carrying handle at each end. The Sunbeam Bread girl was emblazoned on its side. There the pigeons would remain, fattening up, until Baba decided they looked about ready. I had just turned five and was only beginning to make a connection between those slate-gray birds, murmuring and cooing to one another, some with a rainbowlike iridescence where the light hit their necks as they pecked at the sawdust floor of their makeshift coop, and that lovely little chickenlike dark meat my mother occasionally set before us.

→→→

I actually do have a pigeon recipe to share, but first, here's a "pigeonlike" recipe, and it's no ordinary meal. This one's a feast, meant to impress!

Heshweh bi Djaaj
(Roasted Rock Cornish Hens on Heshweh with Laban Sauce)

THE HENS:
3 Rock Cornish hens
¼ cup pomegranate molasses

1. Preheat oven to 450°F. Line a rimmed cookie sheet with aluminum foil, place a wire rack atop it. Spray with cooking spray.
2. Using kitchen scissors, cut each bird in half, starting with the back and dividing it lengthwise, along the spine from tail to neck, then on the other side, snip down from neck to the bottom of the breastbone.
3. Place each half bird, skin side up, on the wire rack, place in oven, and immediately turn the temperature down to 325°F.
4. After 20 minutes, flip the halves, brush with pomegranate molasses. After 20 minutes, flip again, and brush the skin sides with molasses. After another 20 minutes, remove from oven and set aside to rest.

THE LABAN SAUCE:
2 cups plain yogurt
2 tablespoons olive oil
1 tablespoon dried mint
1 tablespoon lemon juice
1 teaspoon salt
½ teaspoon white pepper
1 garlic clove, minced (optional)

In a medium-size bowl, whisk the yogurt and olive oil together. Stir in the remaining ingredients. Cover and chill in the fridge.

THE *HESHWEH*:

4 tablespoons (½ stick) butter
1 small onion, chopped fine
1 garlic clove, minced
1½ pounds ground lamb (or lamb and beef mixed)
1½ teaspoons salt
1 teaspoon black pepper
1 heaping teaspoon allspice
2 heaping teaspoons ground cinnamon
¼ teaspoon nutmeg
½ teaspoon dried mint
1 cup rice
½ cup toasted pine nuts
½ cup toasted slivered almonds
¾ cup chopped parsley, divided
1 cup shredded rotisserie-cooked chicken breast meat (optional)

1. Melt butter in a large fry pan.
2. Add onion and garlic and sauté over medium heat until translucent.
3. Raise heat to medium high, add meat, and sauté.
4. Meanwhile, add a little over 2 cups of water to a separate pan and bring to a boil.
5. When meat is lightly browned, add salt, pepper, allspice, cinnamon, nutmeg, mint, and rice. Stir about 30 seconds, then carefully add 2 cups of the boiling water.
6. Return to a boil, then cover; lower heat and simmer for 15 minutes.
7. Stir in pine nuts, almonds, and ½ cup of the parsley.
8. Stir in chicken breast meat, if using.

ASSEMBLING THE DISH:

1. Plate by mounding the *heshweh* on a large platter.
2. Sprinkle entire dish with the remaining ¼ cup parsley.
3. Arrange the hen halves atop the *heshweh*, giving them a finishing touchup shine of pomegranate molasses.
4. Drizzle the borders of the steaming platter with ice-cold *laban* sauce, and bring to the table with a bowl of *laban* sauce to pass.

Serves 6

Note: Heshweh may be used as a stuffing for fowl or served on the side as dressing. On the plate, it's especially nice served hot and topped with ice-cold yogurt.

→ → →

Armenian Mirkatan (or Persian Khoshab) (page 27) and Siliq Migleh (page 57) would make delicious accompaniments to this feast. As does the following salad.

Fattoush
(Bread Salad)

1 loaf Arabic bread
3 tomatoes
3 cucumbers
Arils of ½ pomegranate
6 scallions, chopped
1 cup parsley, roughly chopped
¼ cup mint leaves, chopped
½ cup Greek olives, pitted
¼ cup olive oil
¼ cup lemon juice
½ teaspoon sugar
1 teaspoon salt
1 teaspoon dried mint
1 to 2 tablespoons za'atar
1½ teaspoons pomegranate molasses
2 large garlic cloves, minced

1. Leave bread out to dry overnight, and/or toast in oven till crisp. Break into bite-sized pieces and set aside. (Or, in a pinch, use store-bought pita chips.)
2. Cut tomatoes into wedges.
3. Peel cucumbers and cut in half lengthwise. Use a spoon to scrape out the seeds. Slice the cucumbers into crescents.
4. In a salad bowl, toss together the tomatoes, cucumbers, pomegranate arils, scallions, parsley, mint leaves, and olives.
5. Place olive oil, lemon juice, sugar, salt, dried mint, za'atar, pomegranate molasses, and garlic in a small jar and shake vigorously. Pour over the salad and place bowl in fridge to chill.
6. Fold bread into salad immediately before serving.

Serves 6

➻➻➻

As promised, here's a pigeon recipe, but one that's versatile enough to work equally well for quail, squab, and young pheasant. I learned of it while visiting Egypt; in Middle Eastern cuisine, the Egyptians are the renowned masters of preparing pigeon.

Hammam Mihsheh
(Stuffed Pigeon)

4 garlic cloves, crushed and minced
1 teaspoon kosher salt
Juice of 2 lemons
4 (1-pound) pigeons
2 tablespoons butter
2 tablespoons olive oil
1 small onion, diced small
Pigeon giblets (heart, gizzard, liver), chopped (or, if preferred, a 2 ounces of ground sausage—Lebanese lemon-lamb sausage would work very nicely)
2 cups #3 bulghur (or you might want to substitute another grain, *freekah*)
1½ teaspoons dried mint
1 teaspoon salt
1½ teaspoons black pepper
3 tablespoons melted butter
4 cups chicken broth, divided
Parsley or cilantro sprigs for garnish

1. Stir garlic and kosher salt into lemon juice and rub the mixture over and into the cavities of the birds. Place in a nonreactive bowl, cover, and let marinate in the fridge for 2 to 3 hours.
2. Preheat oven to 350°F. Heat butter and olive oil together in a large frypan. Add the onion and giblets (or sausage) and cook 10 minutes, stirring occasionally. When the onions are beginning to brown, add the bulghur, mint, salt, and pepper; stir for a couple minutes, then remove from heat and set aside.
3. Remove pigeons from marinade and pat dry. Lightly stuff each bird with a tiny scoop or two of the bulghur, setting aside the rest of the mixture.
4. Truss each bird, closing the cavity with heavy thread and/or skewers and tying the legs together. Brush with melted butter.
5. Place pigeons, breasts up, in a Dutch oven and add 1½ cups of the chicken broth, cover, and set to braise in oven for 1 hour. Baste with cooking liquids and return to oven for another hour.

6. When the birds are nearly done, bring the remaining 2½ cups chicken broth to a boil in a large (2-quart, or so) saucepan. Add the remaining bulghur mixture, return to boil, then lower heat to simmer, cover, and cook until liquid is absorbed, about 30 minutes.

7. Nearing the second hour of braising, test birds for doneness by pricking the thigh to see if juices run clear. If they're still running a little pinkish, return to oven for another 15 minutes.

8. To serve, remove trussing from birds, arrange them on a bed of couscous, and garnish with parsley.

Eighteen 🌿

Murder!

Our radio sat on a table in the front room. It was a wooden, curve-topped model, about the size of a breadbox. A small, keystone-shaped dial lit up when it was turned on, and in keeping with Baba's wishes, the radio stayed on most of the day, steadily pumping English into our day-to-day lives. In the evenings as the windows darkened, the soft amber glow of its dial was a comfort to me, seeming to add a note of kindliness to the rat-a-tat onrush of all those foreign voices.

I didn't start school until I was almost six—kindergarten, for some reason, wasn't an option—so I remember weekdays alone with Mama, "helping" her clean the kitchen after breakfast. ("Finished with that? All right, now wash the table legs with this rag.") In the background would be the chatter and laughter of *Don McNeill's Breakfast Club*, followed by an endless string of soap operas, which as the day progressed were interspersed with news, popular songs, and comedy shorts. During commercials the voices of the announcers seemed to me to project such urgency that I developed an odd concern that if we didn't do what such authoritative, American voices told us to do—buy Bab-O cleanser, say, or drink Postum—we might be sent back to where we came from.

Back to where we came from? What brought up *that* idea? Actually, back then, the idea seemed always to be there, a nagging, low-grade undercurrent of fear all during our first years in America. The words themselves came from the kids we played and quarreled with on the sidewalks and parking lots of our neighborhood, "Go back where you came from!" being only one of their taunts. Another was "Dirty Syrians!" which made me feel ashamed and . . . dirty. Our skin wasn't like theirs, our hair, our eyes. I wished for blue eyes.

My brother may have had similar feelings, but he dealt with them differently. Hotheaded like Baba, and a lot braver than his little brother, he put up his dukes whenever a kid mocked his accent. After a brief fistfight/wrestling match, the matter was settled, and in maybe a day or two everything was usually forgotten, and they were friends again.

But me, I didn't forget. That undercurrent of fear wouldn't let me. Because what if they were right? What if we *didn't* belong? No wonder the authoritarian voice of the radio announcer insisting that we drink Postum sounded to me like a command from America itself.

➤➤➤

Meanwhile, the radio did seem to be having an effect on Mama's struggles to learn English—albeit an unexpected one. Right out of the blue, but always while preoccupied with cooking or some household chore, she would utter aloud something that she'd heard repeatedly on the radio. "All right, Louie, drop da gun, you not-a foolin' anyone," or "An' now . . . *Stella Dallas*," or following a sigh, "'Goodnight Irene.'" Parrotlike, the words seemed to escape her absently, in the middle of kneading dough or roasting an eggplant on the stove burner. They were apropos of nothing, but they *were* English.

There were other unexpected results to learning English from the radio. I remember how my brother and sister and I used to howl with laughter at a character named Mr. Baxter—*baxter* being exactly how Baba pronounced *bastard*, which we knew was a very naughty word. More laughter when advertisers urged listeners to take "the thirty-day Camel test" because Camels were "good for the T-zone," meaning the throat, I would later learn, but the word *T-zone* happens to translate to "their asses" in Arabic. The Christmas I was five, listening to carols on the radio, we all puzzled over what "fa la la . . . la la la la" meant. As for "sle-ep in heav-enly pee-ee-ee," what can I say? We knew we weren't supposed to laugh, but what else could we do?

Later in the day, the radio gave us dramas like *Gang Busters*, *Dr. Kildare*, or *The Shadow*. One of these, *The Fat Man*, was a murder mystery that would become forever etched in my memory. After the announcer recited its signature opening—"a fast-moving criminologist who tips the scales at 237 pounds!"—he would add a touch of menace to his voice as he presented the title of tonight's episode, and whatever the title, it invariably included the word "murder," as in "Murder Plays a Fiddle," or "Murder Takes the Subway." Now it was clear to me that "murder" was a bad thing, but what kind of bad thing, exactly, I had no idea. Having nobody I could ask, I relied on my imagination.

Just as I always imagined Don McNeill as wearing a red bow tie, just as I automatically "saw" Stella Dallas with black bushy hair like Nancy from the comic strip, so I pictured "murder" as a mysterious black ball. Thus, when "Murder Rides the Merry-Go-Round" aired, I saw a carousel pony ridden by . . . a black ball. Not a cutesy cartoon version with arms and legs and a face; no, I saw a black ball about the size of a muskmelon in my dad's store. I saw it perched on a pastel saddle, going up and down to calliope music, or in "Murder Gets a Shave," perched on a barber's chair.

Then, one evening when I was almost five, my uncle Vincent stopped by for a drop-in visit. Like so many of the *ibn Arab* uncles of my growing up, he was actually an elder cousin whom we called "Uncle" out of respect. As he climbed the stairs, I saw he was carrying what looked like a small valise or suitcase. "Get a load of what I just bought on sale," he announced, pausing at the doorway to the stairs. I'd joined my parents in the front room, at the far end of the hall. "Watch this," he said, and took out of the valise something I'd never in my life seen before—a heavy black ball. Laughing, Uncle Vincent slowly rolled the bowling ball down the floor of the hall and into front room, right toward me. I threw my hands up into the air and ran. "Murder!" I screamed. "It's murder! It's murder!"

➳ ➳ ➳

This dish was a favorite of Uncle Vincent's mother, my aunt Yemnah. *Salemlee hal diyat*, we said to show appreciation for such a meal, a blessing on the hands that made it. Back when I'd first moved away from Toledo and was teaching and living alone far away in the Ozarks of Missouri, it's one of the first Middle Eastern dishes I learned to make. I realized then that learning to create these flavors—lamb browned in cinnamon and allspice, Syrian rice, and savory tomato-based sauce—was a way of remembering home and of honoring the work of my mother's hands.

Loubyeh bi Laham
(Green Bean Stew)

1½ tablespoons butter, divided
1½ tablespoons olive oil, divided, plus more as needed
1 pound lamb leg or shoulder cut, cubed and patted dry
1 tablespoon all-purpose flour
1 cup chicken broth, divided
1 medium onion, sliced into crescents
2 garlic cloves, crushed and finely diced
1 teaspoon salt
½ teaspoon black pepper
1 teaspoon ground cinnamon
¼ teaspoon allspice
2 tablespoons tomato paste
2 cans (14.5 ounces) cut green beans, rinsed and drained
1 can (14.5 ounces) diced tomatoes
1 can (14.5 ounces) whole tomatoes

1. With burner on medium high, heat half of the butter (¾ tablespoon) and half of the oil (¾ tablespoon) in a Dutch oven. Sprinkle meat with flour and brown it in batches, adding more oil as needed. Remove meat and set aside. Deglaze pot on high heat with ½ cup of the broth, scraping up browned bits.
2. Add remaining butter and oil (¾ tablespoon each) to the same Dutch oven, sauté onions on medium heat, about 4 minutes. Add garlic, salt, pepper, cinnamon, and allspice.
3. After a minute, stir in tomato paste. Add beans and the meat. Hand crush the whole tomatoes and pour them and their juice over the top. Add the diced tomatoes.
4. Cover and simmer on low heat about 1 hour, stirring occasionally, adding the remaining ½ cup broth, or more or less to adjust thickness of the *zoum* or "gravy." Serve over rice.

Note: A small platter of iced radish slices, buttered and salted, makes a nice complement to this dish.

Serves 4 to 6

Nineteen

Bluffing

My sister, VeeVee, first to go to school, was held back a year because, although she quickly learned to grasp what the teacher was saying, when called on to answer a question, she could give her response only—and correctly, she maintains—in Arabic. The following year my brother narrowly missed also being held back. Not wanting a repeat of VeeVee's experience, Baba cooked up a scheme.

On a hot Sunday afternoon in September, just before the start of the new school year, Baba hung up his white apron and closed the store earlier than usual. He came upstairs to splash water on his face and change his shirt. Then, making sure that the three of us kids were, as he'd earlier directed, all still wearing our Sunday Mass best, he herded us downstairs. On the sidewalk, Baba had the three of us hold hands as we followed behind him to my brother's school.

Saint Patrick's Elementary, operated by the Ursuline nuns, was only a short three or four blocks from the store. But when we reached the school, Baba continued on past; it being a Sunday, the building was closed. Instead he led us down a side street to the nuns' convent-house residence, where he sat us on the front stoop. We complied, having no more of an idea of what he was up to than did the nuns whom we could see peering out at us now through the window lace. Baba kept his back to the window. He sat down on the stoop and drew my brother into his arms. Then, pulling out his red kerchief, he dabbed at his eyes, shook his head side to side, and began to softly moan, just as he did Saturday nights, drinking arak and listening to his 78 rpms of Arabic *atayba* singing. Of course, my sister and brother and I promptly joined in; but even as we bawled away, even I, the youngest, somehow knew that these tears weren't real, that this was some sort of an act. My father's eyes were always a mystery; for me, it was his mouth that gave him away. Anger, sadness, stony indifference, or the fleeting twitch of a half-smile—he couldn't bluff. I could read him by his mouth.

After a few minutes, the door opened, and the principal stepped out, followed by another nun, my brother's teacher. The two of them slowly shook their heads side to side in dismay. The gesture actually made a sound, a twin crackling of their stiffly starched wimples. Next morning, we learned that my brother had been promoted, on a trial basis, to second grade. And the morning after that, the Ursuline residence found on its front stoop a bushel basket of fresh fruit—peaches, nectarines, plums, and just-ripe cantaloupes.

➤ ➤ ➤

In our family, Baba was the disciplinarian, Mama being simply too much of a soft touch. Her approach was to warn us that we would be punished as soon as Baba got home. It was her only threat, but it was all she needed. One of my clearest memories of Monroe Street is of me playing on the sidewalk one Sunday without having changed out of my church clothes as I'd been told to do. Above me I heard the *tik-tik-tik* of my mother's ring on the window glass. I looked up, and there she was in the blue stuffed chair, where she used to sit saying her rosary. She gave me a stern look, and pressing thumb and two fingertips together, she shook her hand at me in the Arabic patience sign, meaning "just you wait." Meaning, of course, Baba.

Baba could get angry and scary loud. And yet when it came to backing up his anger, he usually turned out to be a soft touch too. In other words, he was a bluffer. I learned this when I was very small. My brother and sister and I had done something to infuriate Mama. I don't remember what, but it was bad enough to warrant the ultimate punishment, the Belt. Oh, the hours of dread as the three of us waited for Baba to close the store and come upstairs!

None of us recall the Belt ever actually being used, only the threat of it. Even so, as soon as we heard his footsteps on the stairs, we scattered about the flat, cowering under tables and behind stuffed chairs, while Mama, her fury renewed by his arrival, excitedly told him whatever it was we'd done. *They did WHAT?!* His own anger now ignited, he started after us, herding the three of us into a corner of the kitchen. Slowly, he unbuckled his belt, and slowly, he began to slide it out of its trouser loops.

I don't know what came over me just then, but I stood up out of my cowering crouch, stepped forward, and pointed out to him, "If you take your belt off, Baba, your pants are going to fall down."

He stopped cold. His eyes were fiery with anger, but I kept my own eyes on his mouth. I watched his lip quiver as he struggled to keep it twisted in a scowl. Then he abruptly turned away, letting go a quick wheeze of suppressed laughter.

After that day, whenever my brother or sister was threatened with the Belt, they would shove me in front of them and plead, "Make him laugh! Make him laugh!"

→ → →

Aunt Sophie, Baba's half-sister, could make him laugh, too. In fact, she could make anybody laugh. It wasn't that Sophie's stories and jokes were so funny. They were fairly corny, as I remember. But her delivery, so urgent and high-spirited, got us laughing before she was halfway into the story.

One in particular I remember was about the citizenship process, the judge asking the immigrant, "What flies over the post office, the courthouse, and the state capitol building?" The immigrant's answer, as Sophie delivered it: "De Bidgins!"

Aunt Sophie showed me how to make *bazella*, one of my all-time favorite lamb dishes. Sitting in her kitchen in Detroit about a year after my mother passed, we got to talking about some of the dishes Mama used to cook and how much I wished I'd paid better attention to how she'd made some of them. Before I knew it Aunt Sophie was up and cooking about four different dishes, one after the other, while I followed her around with a pad and pencil. Like Mom, she didn't have recipes written down (neither of them was much of a reader or writer), and the proportions she used were all eyeballed estimates. "Abowd dis much flour," she'd say, showing me her cupped hand, and I would hastily scribble, "Abt. ½ c. flour." Then, looking up again, I'd see her scooping yet another quarter cup of flour and tossing it into the bowl. "Wait Auntie," I protested.

She only chuckled. "Needed a leettle more."

What could I do? I wrote, "¼ c. more flour."

And that's the way it went all afternoon. Me crossing out, inserting, rewriting, while Aunt Sophie moved busily from stove to pantry to sink. Everything she made that afternoon turned out delicious, especially her version of *bazella*, to which, in her memory, I've added a touch or two of my own.

Bazella
(Stew of Lamb and Peas)

1 tablespoon olive oil
2 tablespoons butter
1½ pounds cubed lamb
1 medium onion, chopped
1½ teaspoons salt
4 garlic cloves, minced
½ teaspoon black pepper
1½ teaspoons ground cinnamon
1 teaspoon allspice
1 teaspoon ground coriander
¼ teaspoon nutmeg
¼ teaspoon Aleppo pepper (this spice delivers a medium heat
    with wonderful cuminlike undertones) (optional)
1 cup ¼-inch-thick sliced carrots (about 3 large carrots)
3 tablespoons tomato paste
1 ounce semisweet dark chocolate, grated or broken in bits
1½ cups chicken broth
1 bag (16 ounces) frozen peas

1. Using a Dutch oven or a large, lidded fry pan, bring oil and butter to
   medium-high heat. Brown the lamb cubes. Remove meat and set aside.
2. In the same pan, add onion, sprinkle with salt, and sauté over medium-
   high heat until the onion softens and starts to turn golden (about 10
   minutes). Lower heat to medium, add garlic, and cook a minute or so,
   then add the pepper, cinnamon, allspice, coriander, and nutmeg. Stir and
   cook another minute.
3. Add the Aleppo pepper (if using), carrots, tomato paste, chocolate, and
   broth. Stir. Return the meat to the pan. Stir. Bring to boil, then reduce heat
   and cover. Let simmer 20 minutes.
4. Uncover, let sauce cook down, about 5 minutes. Stir in the peas and cook
   another 2 to 3 minutes. Serve over Riz bi Siriyeh (page 15).

Note: Like *ful bi laham, bazella* is nicely accompanied by a little pot of
ice-cold *laban* to pass.

Serves 6 to 8

Twenty

The Need to See a Man

Although I could literally disarm my father by making him laugh, he still scared me. Maybe because in those early years he was such a stranger to me. Seven days a week, he opened the store early, and seven days a week, he closed it late. His workday started with a predawn stop at the City Market, where he dealt with wholesalers and suppliers. He didn't tramp back up the stairs until past my bedtime; I remember lying under the heavy, quilted *l'hahf* and listening as Mama heated up supper for him.

Fifty-six years old when I was born, he was always an old man to me, always cranky and in poor health. But he was my father, and because of that fact I craved him. Or something like him. There is an old adage: To be a man you need to see a man. Only twice can I recollect, as a small child, ever going anywhere alone with him, just the two of us.

The first time, we were in a shop somewhere, and as the clerk made change at the cash register, he asked Baba if I was his grandson. Immediately Baba pulled me close against the side of his leg. "Whaddya mean?" he said. "This one is *mine!*" The pride in his voice surprised me. I really didn't know he felt that way.

The other time I recall, he brought me along with him on his errands—I don't remember why, probably one of the times Mama was in the hospital. But there we were, Baba and I, early one morning in what must have been the City Market, some of its stalls sheltered by a line of narrow roofs, the rest indoors in a huge barnlike facility. It was still dark out, and I remember the moist, fruity smell of the place, how busy the people around us seemed, the noisy bustle they all made, and Baba holding my hand to keep me out of everyone's way. We walked into another large, barnlike building, this one lit by banks of brighter-than-bright light bulbs, and its cement floor covered in sawdust at least a couple inches thick. Baba told me to stop scuffing it around. I gripped his hand more tightly when a motor abruptly roared to life somewhere in the high ceiling. He turned away from the man he was talking to—I don't remember the man's face, only the blue denim apron he had on—and we all looked up at what appeared to be a moving row of hooks that had begun traveling down a gradually descending conveyor chain. The motor settled into a steady whine as the hooks descended toward us, dangling and swaying to within about six feet above our heads; the hooks looked huge, about the size of my father's hand. Then came the sheep.

They were hanging upside down, each with a hook piercing a tendon on that lower part of the hind leg called the shank. They were silent, or else their bleats were drowned out by the noise of the motor, but it did seem to me they were kicking a little as the chain moved them along. Thinking back, they were probably already dead, or else stunned unconscious, and the movement I saw was caused by the motion of the chain. Turning away, I saw that the man in the denim apron had taken a position about fifteen or so feet down the line from us. He stood with his back to the dangling sheep, and I could see he now held a cloth in one hand, a narrow black knife in the other. As each sheep approached, he methodically half-turned, reached out his knife hand, slit the animal's throat, half-turned back, wiped the blade on the cloth, then turned and cut the next throat in line, turned back, wiped the blade. Receiving the cut, each animal's head immediately seemed to go limp and hang heavier, the open throat bleeding out onto the sawdust, one after the other—turn out—slice—turn in—wipe—next—as the noisy chain yanked them along, heads dangling and bobbling, up through a passageway and on into another room. I don't remember feeling frightened or disgusted, nor even particularly sorry for the animals, although over the years I've looked back on this memory and felt all these things. At the time, I think what I felt most was fascination. I see. *I see.* I was holding my father's hand, and he was showing me how it was done.

➤➤➤

In the butcher shop behind the grocery, I used to watch my father transform entire carcasses as he sawed, cleavered, and carved. His black knife blade had a long silvery edge, and he seemed to enjoy sliding it effortlessly through the white fat and down into the deepest purple-red muscle. Upstairs in the kitchen, Mama cut meat too, preparing a pot roast for our family dinner, cutting a lamb shoulder down to useable portions. While I wouldn't say she was queasy about carving and trimming, I can't say she enjoyed it, either. Many a time she would be sitting at the kitchen table, quietly working away with a knife on a piece of lamb that Baba had sent up to her from downstairs, when suddenly we'd hear her slam the knife down on the table and cry out "Yih!"—not in pain but utter creeped-outedness—at having uncovered an artery or a section of connective tissue, some reminder that this had been a living thing. Then she'd get over it, release a deep breath, and continue carving.

➤ ➤ ➤

This recipe features lamb shanks, one of my favorite cuts, which I enjoy with gratitude—to the sheep, primarily, but also to the butcher.

Bulghur bi Laham
(Cracked Wheat with Lamb)

1½ pounds lamb shanks
2 tablespoons butter, plus extra as needed
2 to 3 cups liquid (water, or broth for extra richness)
2 large onions, thickly sliced
1 can (14.5 ounces) chickpeas, drained and rinsed
1 tablespoon ground caraway
1 teaspoon ground cinnamon
½ teaspoon allspice
1 teaspoon salt, or to taste
1½ cups #3 bulghur
A generous ¼ cup of Laban Sauce (page 93)

1. In a fry pan, brown the shanks in butter. Remove to a Dutch oven, and add enough of the liquid to cover meat. Bring to boil, then cover and lower heat to a simmer.

2. Using fry pan and adding more butter as needed, sauté the onions until transparent. Add prepared onions, chickpeas, caraway, cinnamon, allspice, and salt to the meat. Re-cover and continue to simmer, removing foam as it forms, until the meat is tender (about 35 to 45 minutes).

3. Rinse and drain the bulghur before adding it to the meat. Cover, raise heat to bring to boil, then lower heat to simmer again (more liquid can be added if needed). When liquid is absorbed (about 20 to 30 minutes), the dish is ready to serve.

4. Serve on a large platter, topped with ice-cold *laban* sauce.

Serves 4

Twenty-One

Fish or No Fish

Much of Lebanese cuisine is founded on peasant cookery. You don't find a lot of red meat because throughout the history of the Mediterranean red meat was available to the peasant only rarely, pun notwithstanding; and when there was meat, there was little of it to go around. Many of the heart-healthy aspects of the Mediterranean diet are a result of solving the problem of how to make a little bit of meat go a long way. And how to do it deliciously. Or as William Saroyan once put it, "If you must eat, for God's sake make it good!"

And one way to do that would be to mince what little bit of meat you have and use it primarily to flavor a porridge or soup, like Kibbit Kishik (page 20) or a vegetable stew, as in Loubyeh bi Laham (page 101). Another method would be to combine the meat with a filling starch, like rice, and stuff it into available vegetables, such as eggplant, peppers, or zucchini.

But sometimes, even when there is meat available, you can't use it . . . because you mustn't. Areas of Lebanon have remained Christian throughout the Muslim conquests, and Christianity, like many religions, incorporates into its teachings a number of food restrictions: thus Lent and the meatless Fridays of my growing up.

Meatless Fridays were taken very seriously when I was a child. I was taught—by apparently levelheaded, educated grown-ups—that if I were to die after purposely eating only a single bite of meat on a Friday, God would condemn me to burn in the fires of hell for ever and ever and ever. And ever.

What I *wasn't* taught, but learned on my own years later, was that meatless Fridays—along with many of the other days of fasting and abstinence throughout the liturgical year—were invented by medieval bishops who wanted to bolster markets for various European fishing industries.

And not so long ago and far away, there's this I also learned: during the first decades of the last century, Toledo's many ethnic neighborhoods were populated by a significant number of mostly Roman Catholic Eastern European immigrants, mostly factory workers, who, being paid at the end of the week, enjoyed Friday fish fries at their corner pubs. Also then—as now—northwest Ohio's creeks and its many marshy areas are inhabited by muskrats, semiaquatic rodents that grow fat (and tasty, many claim) on the roots of wetland grasses. So in addition to fish, many of these pubs also featured nuggets of deep-fried muskrat. Friday or not, the men who frequented the pubs didn't care so much, but their women, and their priests, were a different story. On the one hand there was eternal damnation, but on the other hand, well, it just didn't seem fair, tempting good working people week after week with juicy but untouchable morsels of muskrat. The solution? Simple. If a European bishop in the Middle Ages could decree Fridays meatless, then why couldn't an American bishop in 1930s Toledo pronounce the muskrat a fish?

Which he did.

No kidding.

Now some of my sources claim that the decree was established much earlier—back in the 1700s when Europeans first settled the Great Black Swamp of northwest Ohio; others say it began in the early 1900s. Either way, in 1987, Edmund Casimir Szoka, archbishop of Detroit, officially revoked the dispensation, and the muskrat was no longer a fish.

➤➤➤

Siami added to a recipe's name means that the dish has been prepared without meat or meat broth and is therefore suitable for observing the laws of fasting and abstinence.

What follows are a couple of stuffed-vegetable recipes developed over time for when there is no meat at all.

Koosa Mihshi Siami
(Stuffed Zucchini Squash, Vegetarian Version)

THE BASIC VEGETARIAN FILLING:
1 cup uncooked short-grained rice
1 small bunch parsley, finely chopped
5 to 6 scallions, finely chopped
½ of 14.5-ounce can of chickpeas, drained and rinsed
½ cup toasted pine nuts
1 tablespoon lemon juice
1 teaspoon salt
½ teaspoon black pepper

THE SQUASH:
12 to 15 small or medium-sized zucchini squash
1 can (28 ounces) whole tomatoes
3 garlic cloves
2 teaspoons dried mint

1. Mix the filling ingredients together in a large bowl and set aside.
2. Trim off the stem ends of the squash and use a vegetable corer (or a *mankara*—see note below) to hollow out the squash to about ¼-inch thickness. (Tip: Measure how deep you want to go by placing the corer alongside the zucchini and using your thumb to mark the spot; keep your thumb on that spot as you core out the insides.)
3. Stuff each zucchini to about ¾ full with the filling (remember, rice expands as it cooks) and place in a large pan or Dutch oven. Add tomatoes (crushing them with your hand), garlic, and water to cover.
4. Cover pan and let simmer about 45 minutes, sprinkling on the dried mint in the last 5 to 10 minutes.

Serves 6 to 8

NOTES:

- Any yellow or green zucchini will work fine, but if you can find it, use the pale, grayish-green Syrian squash, sometimes called Indian squash.
- I prefer San Marzano canned tomatoes, but Hunt's is very good too!
- A *mankara* is a metal tool available at Middle Eastern markets and online.

➤➤➤

Malfouf Mihshee Siami
(Vegetarian Cabbage Rolls)

THE FILLING:
1 cup #3 bulghur, rinsed and squeezed
1 can (14.5 ounces) of chickpeas, drained and rinsed
2 tomatoes, chopped small
1 small bunch parsley, chopped small
1 medium onion, chopped small
¼ cup lemon juice
¼ cup olive oil
1 teaspoon salt
½ teaspoon black pepper
½ cup pomegranate arils (optional)

THE CABBAGE:
1 large head cabbage
3 garlic cloves, sliced
¼ cup olive oil
1 teaspoon salt
2 teaspoons dried mint
Lemon slices to garnish

1. Mix filling ingredients together in a large bowl and set aside.
2. Core cabbage and reserve core. Blanch cabbage in salted boiling water. As leaves begin to become slightly limp and tender, remove them one at a time. Place in a colander to cool. (See note below.)
3. Use a sharp paring knife to remove the thick center rib from each leaf, cutting the larger leaves in half. Reserve ribs and torn or discarded leaves.
4. Line the bottom of large pan or Dutch oven with the reserved core, ribs, and discarded leaves.
5. On clean towel or cutting board, lay out a leaf, place a scant tablespoon of stuffing along one end, then roll, tucking in the ends as you continue to roll up and away from you. Stack finished rolls in the Dutch oven, placing the layers crosswise to each other, and scatter a few slices of garlic atop each layer. Finally, add oil and salt.

6. Place a heavy dish, inverted, atop the final layer. Fill pot to cover plate with water. Cover pot and bring to a boil, then reduce heat and let cook 25 to 30 minutes.
7. Serve sprinkled with dried mint and garnished with lemon slices.

Note: Instead of steps 2 and 3 above, many cooks prefer to carefully peel away the outer leaves, place them in a plastic bag, and freeze overnight; the next day, they allow leaves to defrost on the counter.

Zucchini and cabbage rolls can be made nonvegetarian by mixing and using this basic meat filling instead:

1 pound ground lamb
1 cup uncooked short-grained rice
1 tablespoon ground cinnamon
1 teaspoon allspice
2 teaspoons salt
½ teaspoon black pepper
1 tablespoon olive oil
1 egg, beaten
Optional: pine nuts, dried mint, finely chopped onion or shallots

➜ ➜ ➜

When I was a young man, I was lucky enough to see Lebanon in its heyday, just before the civil war broke out. As my friend Samir was driving me down the coast road toward Sidon and Tyre, he said that we simply had to stop for lunch at this famous seafood restaurant he knew of where Brigitte Bardot loved to eat on her visits to Lebanon. I was doubtful, of course. But I was also a young man. Brigitte Bardot? Well, lead the way!

The place turned out to be a tiny, shacklike building set out on a projection of the rocky coast. Inside there was room for no more than three tables, and though it was lunchtime, we were the only customers. Brigitte Bardot indeed!

Samir ordered fish for the both of us, and we waited. And waited. Finally, I asked, not too originally, "What's taking so long, are they catching the fish?" Samir must have been waiting for me to ask that very question. "Yes!" he exclaimed. "Wanna see?" and he led me outside to the back of the shack, and there on the rocks stood a couple of boys with what looked like bamboo poles, yanking in these silvery, half-pound-sized fish. Soon, Samir and I were tucking into those little fishes, and they turned out to be not only the freshest but also the best, most delicate-tasting fish I'd ever eaten.

Several years later I was reading *Time* magazine about the civil war raging in Lebanon, and it mentioned that because of the turmoil, actress Brigitte Bardot was saddened that she could no longer visit her favorite restaurant near Sidon, where they sent boys out to catch the fish while you waited.

Samek Harrarah
(Spicy Fish)

1½ teaspoons salt
4 fish steaks, about 1½ inches thick (such as salmon, bass, or grouper)
¼ cup olive oil, plus more if needed
1 medium onion, sliced
4 garlic cloves, minced
¾ cup chopped fresh cilantro
1 teaspoon ground cumin
Boiling water, about 2 cups
Juice of 2 lemons
¾ teaspoon cayenne pepper

1. Rinse, pat dry, and salt fish steaks.
2. Heat oil in a large fry pan. Briefly sauté steaks on both sides and remove to a plate.
3. Sauté onion, garlic, cilantro, and cumin for 2 or 3 minutes, adding more oil if needed, and stirring so the garlic doesn't burn. Drain off excess oil.
4. Place fish steaks on top of the onions in the fry pan, then carefully pour in boiling water until it comes halfway up the sides of the steaks. Let simmer 15 minutes.
5. Mix together lemon juice and cayenne. Carefully transfer steaks to platter. Pour lemon juice mixture over them.

Serves 4

Note: This dish is best served at room temperature with *taratoor* sauce drizzled or on the side. (Recipe follows.)

➤ ➤ ➤

Taratoor Sauce
(Lebanese "Tartar" Sauce)

3 tablespoons tahini
3 tablespoons water
3 tablespoons lemon juice
3 sprigs parsley, finely chopped
1 garlic clove, minced and mashed with 1 teaspoon of coarse salt (or ½ teaspoon garlic powder)
Salt, to taste
¼ cup toasted pine nuts (optional)

1. Mix tahini with water until mixture whitens and becomes smooth.
2. Stir in lemon juice, parsley, and garlic. Taste for salt; add as needed.
3. Sprinkle with pine nuts.

Kummuniyeh
(Baked Fish with Cumin)

Butter or spraying oil, for greasing
¼ cup olive oil
2 large sweet onions, thickly sliced
1½ teaspoons salt, divided
2 teaspoons ground cumin
4 garlic cloves, thinly sliced
1 bulb fennel, diced small
1 can (15 ounces) tomato purée
½ cup water
1 teaspoon black pepper
4 half-pound filets of any firm white fish (such as cod or mahi mahi)
1 large tomato, thickly sliced
Juice of 1 lemon
½ cup chopped parsley

1. Preheat oven to 350°F. Using butter or spray, grease a 9-by-12-inch baking dish. Set aside.
2. Heat olive oil in a large fry pan, add onions, ½ teaspoon of the salt, and cumin. Sauté on medium, stirring frequently, until the onions start to turn golden, about 6 to 8 minutes. Lower heat to medium low and stir in the garlic. After a minute or so, remove to a plate using slotted spoon.

3. Add fennel to the oil still in the fry pan and sauté on medium heat about 5 to 6 minutes, to soften.
4. Return onions to the fry pan, stir in tomato purée, water, another ½ teaspoon of the salt, and pepper.
5. Raise heat to medium high, and stirring frequently, reduce liquid until contents of the pan are thickened almost to a paste.
6. Rinse fish fillets, place in the baking dish, and sprinkle with the remaining ½ teaspoon of salt. Pour sauce over the fish, smooth with a spatula.
7. Tightly cover the dish with foil and bake for 20 minutes; remove foil and bake another 20 minutes. Remove from oven, sprinkle with lemon juice and parsley.

Serves 4

Twenty-Two

Telling Time

The summer I was five years old my father moved our family out of the flat above the store and we left Monroe Street with its bars and punch-drunk bums for a house in a real neighborhood. Prescott Street, maybe a mile beyond the edge of downtown, wasn't exactly upscale, but there were sidewalks and lawns and families with kids our age. The closest parochial school was Rosary Cathedral, and as summer drew to a close, I remember feeling bad for my brother and sister, who were apprehensive about starting at their new school. I watched them gather their lunch boxes and pencil cases and walk off to school together. Poor Aboody and VeeVee. I somehow had the notion that school was their thing, exclusively, and not mine.

Later that same morning, I should have been suspicious when I saw Baba's green Chrysler pull to the curb. He never came home from the store during the day. Even so, Mama didn't seem surprised. She put lunch out for us, and after we ate, Baba told me to c'mon, get in the car with him. Mama made sure my hair was combed and my clothes were clean, then off my father and I went. Where to? Never mind.

We took the short ride up Ashland to Collingwood. In another minute or two, Baba pulled into the cathedral school parking lot. Uh-oh, I thought, Aboody and VeeVee must be in some sort of trouble. One of the nuns helped Baba fill out a series of forms by asking him questions and writing down his answers. I'd never seen a nun up close before. She had a man's name, Sister Richard, and she sort of looked like a man, with a square jaw and the smudge of a mustache. Finished with the forms, Sister Richard led us to a room filled with other children my age. They were all sitting in rows of attached little desks, faces forward, hands folded. Waiting. For what?

Baba grunted, "Humph," as if to say *That's done*, then, holding his fedora hat behind him in both hands, he turned around and casually walked out of the room.

I stood stunned a moment, then ran out of the room and down the hall after him. "BA-BA-A-A-A!"

"No, you stay dere!" he said in English, brushing me away with his hat.

Why was he speaking in English? To *me*? I dodged his hat and grabbed onto a pant leg.

"G'wan, now, leggo!" he said, untangling my fingers, prying my arms from his knee. I lunged out again, but by now two nuns had hold of me. Wriggling in their grip, I heard the echoing slam of the school door closing heavily after my father.

Back then I understood English more than I could speak it. Well enough, anyway, to understand Sister Richard when she shook her finger in my face: "If you don't stop crying I'll give you something to cry about!"

Well, that seemed to do the trick, I did stop crying—just like that. I had no idea what that "something to cry about" might be, but it didn't sound good. Also, I was making a scene, and these kids my age were all looking at me.

I dried my tears and endured that awful day. Trapped, like my brother and sister before me. Later that afternoon, Aboody and VeeVee walked me home, chattering about their day, which apparently had gone far better than mine. I told them that I was sure glad it was over and done with. "What do you mean over and done?" That was when they told me I had to do this all over again tomorrow.

What? To this day I remember the very spot on the sidewalk on Ashland Avenue where I stopped cold. *What?*

How could I have been so clueless? How was it I felt that school was for my brother and sister and not for me? I don't know where I got that idea, but I'm pretty sure nobody ever told me otherwise. Probably because nobody thought they *had* to. Baba must have figured he'd just take me to school, and presto, I'd fit right in!

Which, ultimately, I did. In fact, I more than fit in at school, I thrived. Especially after I was reassigned to Sister Barbara's first grade. Sister Barbara was a young woman with big, kind eyes and a chubby face, and she was smart, she knew things that she wanted to show me. For Sister

Barbara's sake, I wanted to learn them. At her urging, I quickly worked my way up from Blue Bird to Red Bird—which was the highest reading group. She'd told me I could do it with only a little more practice, and she was right. By Christmas, there I was, peeking ahead in my Red Birds workbook at the section on clocks and numbers, excited by the knowledge that someday soon I would learn how to tell time.

➤➤➤

Sometimes I wonder just exactly what information Dad had given when I was first signed up at cathedral school. I never had a birth certificate; I didn't even have a birthday! In a drawer in the dining room buffet there was a church document, written in Arabic, that supposedly stated that I'd been baptized in November 1944. Which, logically, was the same as the month of my birth because with the Old Country's high infant-mortality rates, babies were brought to the church and baptized as soon as possible. But as for the actual *day* of my birth, or for that matter my sister's birth, or my brother's? Our parents didn't know . . . and they didn't really care. One yellowed piece of paper, most likely copied from a parish ledger, assigned us each a birth month and year. And that's it. We didn't even have middle names!

I turned four when my mother said I was four. Likewise, I turned five when she said I was five. Since my brother and sister and I didn't have birthdays, we never had birthday parties . . . until we started school. First my sister VeeVee was assigned a birthday, then my brother. I have no memory of how they got theirs, but I do remember the day I got mine. It was the year I started school, and Jacky Quinn, my first school friend, had invited me to play at his house on his birthday. It was a play-date more than a party, but there was cake and candles, and I wanted the same for my birthday. So, when my mother told me I was turning six, I asked if I could invite Jacky over for my birthday. Mama said Sunday—which that year happened to fall on the fifth—would be the best day for the party.

"So that's my birthday, then. November the fifth."

But a year later when I wanted to celebrate on November the fifth, Mama said Monday the fifth was a school night and that Friday would be my birthday. I was in second grade by then and could read a calendar. "But Friday is November the *ninth*," I protested.

"Yes," Mama said. "So, Friday is your birthday."

We were in the kitchen and she was cranking wet clothes through the wringer attached to the tub of the washing machine, a procedure I never tired of watching. "So which day was I born on, the fifth or the ninth?"

Sometimes Mama shrugged off unimportant things with a lifting of one eyebrow, sometimes with a little backhanded wave, and sometimes a dismissive *Yallah ba'ah!* which could translate to something like "Let's move on, already!" or "Forget about it!"

For this she gave me only the eyebrow, then continued wringing the wash.

➤➤➤

My first school lunch box, emblazoned with the image of Hopalong Cassidy and his white horse, Topper, was, I thought, very American looking. On the outside, anyway. On the inside was another story. Instead of the baloney sandwich with potato chips that I preferred, what Mama packed me was, more often than not, leftovers from yesterday's supper—slices of roasted chicken breast drizzled with a lemony tahini sauce and wrapped in pita bread, diamonds of kibbeh, stewed eggplant even, which she'd somehow stuffed into the Hopalong Cassidy thermos!

Among the many stewed eggplant variations, Tabagh Rohou is a favorite choice. In Arabic *roh* means "spirit," and *tabagh* means "cook," so the name translates to "the spirit of the cook." It's called that, I think, because its recipe, popular throughout the Middle East, is so widely open to interpretation that every chef and home cook who tries it ends up individualizing the dish by adding a touch of their own preference, a taste of their own spirit. My mother's touch in the recipe below is the lamb shanks; mine is the *snobar*, or pine nuts.

Tabagh Rohou
(Stewed Eggplant)

1 large eggplant
1 tablespoon kosher salt
¼ cup olive oil
1 large onion, roughly chopped in large pieces
2 lamb shanks, sawn in two, crosswise, by the butcher
2 garlic cloves, chopped
1 can (28 ounces) whole tomatoes
1 can (14.5 ounces) chickpeas, drained and rinsed
1¾ cups water
1 teaspoon salt
¼ teaspoon black pepper
2 teaspoons dried mint
¼ cup toasted pine nuts

1. Peel and cube eggplant, sprinkle with kosher salt, and set aside to drain its liquid in a colander, about 20 minutes.
2. Meanwhile, heat oil to a shimmer in the bottom of a Dutch oven. Add the onion and sauté lightly 3 to 4 minutes. Using a slotted spoon, remove onion and set aside.
3. Sauté the shanks in the same oil over medium-high heat, about 5 to 7 minutes.
4. Lower the heat to medium low, stir in the garlic, and place the onions atop the lamb shanks. Hand crush the tomatoes and place atop the onions.
5. Rinse kosher salt from eggplant and spread cubes atop the tomatoes.
6. Spread chickpeas atop the eggplant cubes.
7. Add water, raise heat to medium.
8. Sprinkle with salt, pepper, dried mint, and pine nuts.
9. Bring to a boil, cover, and lower heat enough to maintain a slow simmer for 2 hours.
10. Serve over rice.

Serves 4

➤➤➤

Here is a sweet lunch box snack, or when dessert is "Just a bite, please."

Ajwa Mihsheh
(Stuffed Dates)

12 fresh Medjool dates
½ cup cream cheese or *puck* (*areeshee*—available online and at Middle Eastern markets)
½ cup toasted pine nuts

SPRINKLE MIXTURE:
2 teaspoons brown sugar
1 teaspoon ground cinnamon
½ teaspoon cayenne pepper
3 tablespoons chopped fresh mint leaves
1 tablespoon Aleppo pepper

GARNISH:
Sprig or 2 of mint

1. Place fresh dates in fridge for a few hours to firm up.
2. Halve and pit each date.
3. Fill each half with cream cheese and arrange on a platter.
4. Dot each piece with 3 to 4 pine nuts.
5. In a small bowl, combine ingredients for sprinkle mixture, then dust each date with mixture.
6. Sprinkle the chopped mint leaves over all.
7. Garnish with mint sprigs and serve.

Serves 6

Twenty-Three

The Evil Eye

Up until the start of seventh grade, I remained pretty much a rule follower at school. But then, nearing my twelfth birthday, I felt a change coming over me. My body, my thoughts, my very personality. Looking back, I can see now that of course it was puberty. Burgeoning sexuality driving my story just like those other stories of horrific transformation, the Wolfman, Jekyll and Hyde, the Cat People. One minute I was sitting there, hands folded on my desk like the altar boy I was, and the next minute I was playing the room for laughs, making faces behind Sister Evangelista's back, imitating her ducklike waddle, sassing to her face with under-the-breath, ventriloquized backtalk. I had become the class clown. The girls in class—my primary audience—responded with appreciative giggles. Sister did her best to make me pay dearly for those giggles. She stood me in the corner, she stood me in the hall, she sent me to the principal's office, she denied me recess and kept me after school dusting blackboard erasers. None of it had any effect on my behavior. "Bold as brass," Sister concluded. So, finally, she resorted to administering the clicker.

The clicker. Each Ursuline nun carried one, a device made of two slats of wood about an inch wide and six inches long attached by rubber bands over a spring hinge, so that when the thumb pressed the top slat down and let go, the device produced a loud click. Clickers were used to signal us when to kneel in church or when a line of us in the hall was to stop, get going again, turn. The clicker was also a handy tool of punishment, used to deliver a smack atop some misbehaving boy's noggin (never a girl's), or to slap-redden his upturned palms. Because of me, Sister Evangelista began to wear her clicker at the ready, tucked into the cincture around her waist, like a gat.

Sister Evangelista was one of the older nuns teaching at cathedral school. Somewhat hard of hearing, she also had a problem with her vision that prevented her from looking toward the classroom's bright bank of windows without shading her eyes. A gesture, by the way, that I took great delight in mocking. Sister also had what I now realize must have been tinnitus, because she heard humming that wasn't there. "Where's that humming coming from? Who's humming?" That's all she had to say to get me and a couple of my cronies to actually begin humming. It was practically foolproof. All you had to do was shrug, sit back, look innocent, and breathe through your nose. As you hummed.

Today, looking back through the lens of my own career as a teacher, it's more than clear to me what a pain in the behind I'd been. Sister Evangelista had fifty-six students in her classroom. Fifty-six. A half-dozen of whom—sent to us that year from another school—shared a variety of physical, behavioral, and emotional challenges. And with no coteacher to help her out, no assistant. No Ritalin or Adderall, either. Just her and the fifty-six of us.

Clicker? It's a wonder she didn't use a baseball bat.

➤➤➤

I've sometimes wondered whether the stress caused some of the good sisters to end up paying an emotional or mental-health price. How else to explain the "White Pigeon" story, which was like an urban legend. Everybody in cathedral school had heard about how one morning during the Pledge of Allegiance, a white pigeon flew across the parking lot from the church to the school and alit on the classroom windowsill. The sister was thunderstruck by the sight, gasping that this had to be a visitation from God, the embodiment of the Holy Ghost (in those pre–Vatican II days, it was "Ghost" and not "Spirit"). She made the class get down on their knees, bless themselves with the sign of the cross, and pray to the white bird.

At home, it was no huge jump from such a mindset to my family's own superstitions. Mama, for instance, told the story of Saint Maron, whose holiness was revealed when he draped his cloak over a sunbeam and it hung there. And don't get me started on the Evil Eye, a curse you can cast unintentionally! Without even knowing! Luckily there was a blue bead you could get, painted to resemble an eye, that protected you. So did tiny pieces of cloth touched by the relics of saints when safety-pinned to your undershirt. If there was a vial of holy water handy, prepare to get sprinkled. And there was always a vial of holy water handy. My mother kept hers in a little jar in a drawer of the dining room buffet. Her supply came from the miraculous shrine of Our Lady of Consolation in Carey, Ohio, where the families of the *ibn Arab* from Michigan to Pennsylvania made pilgrimages every year. When that supply ran out (usually meaning it had been a tough year), we resupplied at the font in the Rosary Cathedral across the street.

Once when I was nine or ten, I won a set of steak knives in a school raffle. I was so excited to bring them home to Mama. But instead of being delighted with the present, she glanced once into the gift box, then quickly replaced the lid and set the box on a high shelf. Later, when Baba came home after closing the store, he sat down to his supper, and Mama called me into the kitchen. While I stood by, she brought down the box and showed Baba the knives. His face turned pale. "Zuzu gave you these?" he asked. "Quick, give him ten cents!" Mama hurried to the change jar, fished out a dime, and pressed it into my hand. How was I to know that giving a knife as a gift cursed the relationship to be cut? But by giving me the dime, she changed the transaction: now the steak knives became no longer a gift but a purchase.

So, although Baba openly scoffed at any and all forms of religiosity, superstitions seemed to be a different matter. For example, Baba carried a miniature purselike packet, the *djrab il khirdee*, in the area of his left armpit on a string that ran around his neck and shoulder. I saw it only once, when Baba was undressing. It looked to be the size and shape of a small banana wrapped in white adhesive tape. It contained, he claimed, a piece of the True Cross, and if he ever lost it, he would lose all his luck.

I saw the *djrab il khirdee* only that one time, and never again. Because sometime over the years, he ended up losing it. Tucked into his armpit, clamped next to his heart, wrapped in an entire roll of tape, and yet— whether True Cross or not—he lost it.

→→→

Speaking of magic, this recipe was one of my mother's specialties.

Yagneh Sbinakh
(Lebanese Spinach Stew)

2 tablespoons olive oil, divided
2 tablespoons butter, divided
2 medium onions, diced
1 pound ground lamb (or beef . . . or 1 can [14.5 ounces] chickpeas
    for vegetarian)
Salt and black pepper
2 teaspoons allspice, divided
2 teaspoons ground cinnamon, divided
4 teaspoons ground coriander, divided
4 to 5 garlic cloves, mashed
¼ cup toasted pine nuts, divided
1 bunch cilantro, roughly chopped
3 packages (10 ounces) of frozen chopped spinach, thawed,
    drained, and squeezed
1 can (14.5 ounces) chicken (or vegetable) stock
Juice of 2 lemons, divided
¼ cup pomegranate arils

1. In a large skillet on medium heat, mix 1 tablespoon of the oil and 1
   tablespoon of the butter. Add onions and fry till transparent (about 5
   minutes).
2. Add lamb, a pinch of salt and pepper, and 1 teaspoon each of the allspice,
   cinnamon, and coriander, and cook till the meat is browned. Drain and
   divide in half.
3. In another, larger pan or Dutch oven, heat the remaining 1 tablespoon of
   the oil and remaining 1 tablespoon of the butter, add garlic, 2 teaspoons
   of the ground coriander, and half of the pine nuts, and stir over medium
   heat for 1 minute.
4. Add ½ of the meat mixture to the Dutch oven, then the cilantro; spinach;
   chicken stock; half of the lemon juice; the remaining 1 teaspoon of the
   allspice, cinnamon, and coriander; and a pinch of salt and pepper. Bring
   to a boil, then cover and simmer on low heat, 15 minutes.
5. Serve on a platter over rice, sprinkled with the rest of the meat mixture
   (rewarmed), the remaining pine nuts, pomegranate arils, and the
   remaining lemon juice.

Serves 6

Twenty-Four

Jedbeh Arabiyeh

Maybe my parents' birth culture was so steeped in fearful superstitions and cockeyed remedies because that culture was so lacking in rational education; and superstitions are often only methods (albeit misguided) of filling gaps in our knowledge. For a while we received an Arabic language newspaper that came from Detroit every week. I used to watch my mother struggle to read it, squinting in concentration, lips quietly working to form words. Not even reading, more like deciphering. The fact that she was literate at all—in both Arabic and French—was a testament to the generosity of the Salesian Sisters, who ran a mission school in the Christian Quarter; for almost three years, her parents had managed to send her there. Between the nuns and her beloved uncle the priest, she developed a lifelong respect for learning.

But reading also mystified her. While she was proud that I did well in school, it could unnerve her to see me just sitting there, quietly absorbed in a book. To her mind, I was staring steadily at an inanimate object in my hands, a thing no different from a stone or a block of wood. My lips were not moving, only my eyes, steadily scanning left to right, left to right, as if in a trance. Then, if I happened to break the silence with a sudden chuckle at something funny that I'd just read, she'd sign-of-the-cross me three times quick. Why? To ward off demonic possession. Staring intently at an inanimate object and suddenly bursting into laughter must have looked to her like a form of possession. Which, in a way, reading is.

So, considering her background, it's no wonder Mama had such a hard time those first few years in America, mistaking gas stations for art museums, stumbling on escalators, distrusting strangers who only wanted to help. Then as now, it's no small handicap to be raised poor and female in an Arab country. And yet that birth culture was also rich in peasant traditions of hospitality and neighborliness. And despite all the superstitions and cockeyed remedies, there was also something I've come to identify as an underlying current of common sense. My mother's mind was keen, and she had the savvy to recognize pretentiousness for what it was (something she laughingly called *jedbeh Arabiyeh*, or "Arabic tall tales"). Her favorite retort to bs from any of us kids was "*Shookh ou nahm!*" literally, "Pee and go to bed!" She had a sharp sense of humor, too, and she knew how to tell a good bedtime story.

In fact, both my parents were storytellers. Unlike Mama, my father "never saw even one day inside a school room." Which is why, I think, he always held books and education in such high regard. As a youngster in America, he'd managed somehow to learn to read . . . but just barely. The only writing of his I ever saw was the overly elaborate looping of his signature. Of course, Baba, being Baba, never doubted his own intelligence. ("If I wen' to school, just think how far I woulda got!") I think it was with a touch of envy that he watched us kids grind through our homework, and it pleased him to show how he could do my high school algebra problems without paper or pencil, all in his head. When I was stumped by train B going west at x miles per hour, or by a grocer ordering x minus y pecks of oranges, Baba would frown up at the ceiling and think a moment. Then his frown would vanish, and he'd blurt out the correct answer. But *how* had he arrived at that answer? He didn't know. He could only shrug.

Because my parents did have little to no schooling, and because they did come from a culture crawling with myths and superstitions, we kids learned to be cautious, if not outright skeptical, of what they told us. For example, once when I was in fifth grade, my father lay listening from his sickbed at the other end of the sunroom while my sister helped me study for a history test.

"What explorer sailed to America," VeeVee read from my homework sheet, "almost five centuries *before* Columbus?"

An easy one. "Leif Erikson," I replied.

"Who?" Baba struggled to sit himself up.

"The Viking guy."

"*Tch!*" He made the single tsk sound that, in Arabic, means "no."

"Who then?"

"The *Lebanese* discovered America. We come here first!"

"Yeah?" Eye roll between my sister and me. "Uh-huh."

"You betcha! An' we come here a coupla *thousand* years before Columbus!"

"Okay, Baba." What else could my sister and I say? He was our dad. And he'd never been to school.

That happened in the late 1950s. Fast forward to the mid-1990s, I'm living in Iowa and I open the *Des Moines Register* one morning and read that university scholars are studying artifacts unearthed just north of us, up in Minnesota—*Minnesota!*—that appear to have been left by ancient Phoenician sailors who supposedly reached Lake Superior via the Saint Lawrence River. The Phoenicians are, of course, the ancestors of the modern Lebanese.

Another example? I was in sixth grade, and my mother saw me walk into the kitchen with a new book from the Kent Branch Library. The cover showed a battle scene dominated by a mounted warrior in Greek armor. She asked what the book was called.

"*Alexander the Great.*" I figured I'd have to go on to explain who he was, but no need, she already knew the name.

"*Iskandar al Dukarnain,*" she said in Arabic (Alexander the Two-Horned).

"Two-Horned?"

"*Ma'loum!*" (Most truly taught!) "He had horns coming out of his head."

"Really, Ma?"

"Like on a sheep. They came out here," she pointed to her temples, "then down around his ears like this."

"Uh-huh." Eye roll.

Fast forward twenty-some years. I happened to be paging through a book about ancient coins and stopped at the enlarged picture of one coin in particular, a silver piece discovered in Damascus—my mother's home city—and struck around the time that Alexander the Great had invaded Egypt. The coin depicted the head of Alexander, and coming out of his temples and curled down around his ears were the ram's horns of the god Amun-Ra.

➻➻➻

Dad had a pair of cronies, the two Georges we called them, who would visit regularly, usually on Sunday afternoons, usually bringing a box of R. G. Dun cigars. They sat with Dad in the living room, and Mama would serve them arak or Arabic coffee. As soon as the three men lit up, she would retire to the kitchen, closing the door against the smoke.

Sometimes on a Sunday afternoon I would already be there, doing my homework on the kitchen table, and the two of us would listen. You'd think my dad and the two Georges would mostly reminisce past times, maybe discuss politics or current affairs—gossip even. But no. Almost always their conversation took off on quasiphilosophical tangents, going from how closely one of their cousins was related to another cousin and somehow winding up trying to figure the begats in the Old Testament, which I knew for a fact only one of them could have ever read, my dad and the other George both being semiliterate at best. But that never kept them from loudly defending some opinion or other about whether Jonah was fated to be thrown overboard, or whether Lot's wife's daughter could be considered a second cousin to Abraham. Being old men, Dad and the two Georges naturally discussed a number of health issues, too. One such conversation I particularly remember had to do with whether or not a baby's urine was a good wash for cleansing the eyes. Mama, sitting across from me at the kitchen table, would end up pressing her apron to her face, as she gasped and trembled with suppressed laughter.

➤➤➤

Sunday afternoons were for visiting and being visited. When you stopped by someone's house you never showed up empty-handed; custom dictated that the visitor present the hostess with something—a small dish of baklava, stuffed dates, maybe tomatoes, if they were in season, or maybe just a swathe of herbs fresh-picked from your garden. But something. In return you would expect to be served something as well: coffee or tea, a sweet to nibble on. If your visit was unexpected, possibly even the cookies you walked in with.

Here are recipes for a few of the "little somethings" you might have on hand to serve when company drops by on a Sunday afternoon. The first, *mouhalabiyeh*, was introduced to Medieval Europe by French crusaders who called it *le blanc deSiree*, or the Syrian white dish. Syrian immigrants (my mother included) brought this recipe with them to America. Sometimes compared to panna cotta or Bavarian cream, *mouhalabiyeh* has a unique flavor that arises from a balance of orange-blossom water, pistachios, cinnamon, coconut milk, and syrup of rose petals. My daughter Katie, a wonderful cook and our family foodie par excellence, claims it's one of the tastiest dishes she's ever had.

Mouhalabiyeh
(Creamy Rose Confection)

1¼ cups milk
½ cup cream (or half-and-half)
1 can (13.5 ounces) coconut milk
1 cup sugar
5 tablespoons cornstarch diluted in ¼ cup water
Zest of 1 orange
1 teaspoon vanilla extract
½ teaspoon ground cardamom
Pinch of salt
2 tablespoons rose water or orange-blossom water
½ cup chopped pistachios
½ cup pomegranate arils
Rose-petal syrup

OPTIONAL TOPPINGS:
Sprinkle of ground cinnamon
Sprinkle of nutmeg
½ cup toasted shredded coconut flakes

1. In a saucepan, combine milk, cream, and coconut milk. Stir sugar into liquid, and bring to a boil over medium heat; stir regularly to prevent scorching.
2. As liquid starts to boil, turn heat down to low, and continually stirring, add the cornstarch and water mixture.
3. Next, whisk in the orange zest, vanilla extract, cardamom, and salt, and cook on low to thicken (2 to 5 minutes).
4. Remove from heat, and stir in rose water.
5. Ladle into a pie pan or into small bowls for individual servings; let cool and refrigerate about 2 to 4 hours.
6. When firm, top each bowl with pistachios, pomegranate arils, and a drizzle of rose-petal syrup.
7. Add any or all of the optional toppings.

Serves 6 to 8

→→→

Tefah bi Jallab
(Rose-Flavored Apples)

THE SYRUP:
2 cups sugar
1 cup water
1 teaspoon fresh lemon juice
2 teaspoons *jallab* (see note below)

THE FILLING:
½ cup chopped dried apricots
2 tablespoons chopped candied ginger
½ cup golden raisins
Rind of 1 lime cut into strips

THE APPLES:
2 tablespoons butter, melted
4 large green apples (Granny Smiths), halved crossways and cored with a
   melon baller
½ cup cream

TO MAKE THE SYRUP:
1. Place sugar then water in a small pan, without stirring (lest the sugar
   crystalize).
2. Heat to boiling. Let boil about 5 minutes, then add the lemon juice and
   stir. Continue to simmer about 10 more minutes.
3. Remove from heat, and stir in the *jallab*. Let cool.

TO MAKE THE APPLES:
1. Preheat oven to 350°F.
2. Combine filling ingredients in a medium bowl.
3. Brush a deep ovenproof dish with melted butter.
4. Place 1 tablespoon of filling into each apple cavity. Place apples in baking
   dish, and spoon syrup over apples. Cover and bake 20 minutes, basting
   occasionally.
5. Serve with cream drizzled over.

Note: Jallab is a fruit syrup made of grape molasses, grenadine syrup, and rose
water, then smoked with Arabic incense. It is available online and at Middle
Eastern markets.

Serves 4

➻➻➻

Namurrah

(Farina Cakes)

3 tablespoons tahini
4 cups farina (or Cream of Wheat)
3¼ cups sugar, divided
1¼ cups clarified butter (or 2½ sticks butter, melted)
1¼ cups plain yogurt
½ teaspoon baking soda
1 tablespoon baking powder
Pinch of salt
1 tablespoon vegetable oil
1 tablespoon plus 2 teaspoons rose water, divided
25 to 30 pine nuts or blanched almond slivers, toasted
1 teaspoon fresh lemon juice

1. Preheat oven to 375°F.
2. Grease a baking pan (about 9-by-13 inches) with the tahini.
3. In a large bowl, mix together well the farina, 1¼ cup of the sugar, and butter until fairly smooth.
4. In another, smaller bowl, mix together yogurt, baking soda, baking powder, salt, vegetable oil, and 1 tablespoon of the rose water. The mixture will foam up a bit. That's good.
5. Add yogurt mixture to the farina bowl and mix well, using hands.
6. Spread mixture into baking pan. Use a knife to score the top of the batter into 24 (more or less) diamond-shaped servings. Place a pine nut into the center of each diamond.
7. Bake till golden brown (30 to 40 minutes). It can easily overbrown, so keep a careful eye toward the end. Remove from oven and let cool 15 minutes.
8. While cakes bake, prepare syrup. Place the remaining 2 cups of sugar then 1 cup of water in a small pan, without stirring (lest the sugar crystalize). Heat to boiling. Let boil about 5 minutes, then add the lemon juice and stir. Continue to simmer about 10 more minutes. Remove from heat, and stir in the remaining 2 teaspoons of rose water. Let cool.
9. After cakes have cooled 15 minutes, drizzle syrup over the top and cut into the diamond scoring.

Serves 24

➜ ➜ ➜

Rizb Haleeb
(Rice Pudding)

After a long day at cathedral school, it was always a joy to come home, look in the fridge, and find a tray of Mom's little dessert dishes filled with this soothing after-school snack.

4½ cups milk
½ cup arborio or short-grain rice
2 eggs, beaten
3 tablespoons cornstarch
½ to ¾ cup sugar
¼ teaspoon salt
Zest of 1 orange
½ teaspoon vanilla or orange-blossom water
½ cup chopped pistachios
Ground cinnamon to sprinkle, about 1 teaspoon

1. Using medium saucepan and medium heat, bring milk to just boiling. Stir in rice. Lower heat and simmer for 30 minutes, stirring occasionally.
2. Place eggs, cornstarch, sugar, salt, and orange zest in a small bowl and stir until smooth.
3. Temper the eggs by stirring in 4 or 5 tablespoons of the hot milk, 1 spoonful at a time, to warm the egg mixture. Then pour contents of small bowl into the milk mixture while stirring. Simmer a minute or so more till thickened.
4. Remove from heat and stir in vanilla. Pour into ramekins. Cover each with plastic wrap and chill in fridge.
5. Before serving, sprinkle chopped pistachios and/or cinnamon over the top.

Serves 6

➤➤➤

Awamat

On the eve of the Feast of the Epiphany, which Christian Lebanese celebrate on January 6, flour-based sweets are prepared, the tradition being that on this night everything is blessed, and dough will rise without yeast. To ensure prosperity and good luck for the coming year, a silver coin is inserted into a lump of the dough, which is then placed in a cloth bag and hung from a tree branch. This tradition is called *Dayem*, which near as I can translate, means "forever and ever."

The following recipe is one of the most favored Epiphany treats.

Lebanese Crispy Doughnuts

THE DOUGHNUTS:
2 cups all-purpose flour
3 tablespoons cornstarch
2 teaspoons dry yeast
¼ cup warm water
1 tablespoon sugar
1 teaspoon orange-blossom water
1 teaspoon vanilla extract

Beat all doughnut ingredients together until smooth, like pancake batter, and set aside 1 hour to rise.

THE SYRUP:
2 cups sugar
¾ cup water
¼ cup lemon juice

Place all syrup ingredients together in a small saucepan. Bring to a boil for 1 minute or so, then let cool.

THE PROCESS:
1. Heat vegetable oil about ¾ to 1 inch deep in a deep pan set to medium high.
2. Wet a teaspoon to scoop the batter 1 teaspoon at a time. Take care not to crowd the pan. Turn doughballs till golden on both sides. Remove from oil and blot on paper towels.
3. When they are cool enough to handle, mound the doughballs on a plate and douse them with cold syrup.

Makes about 1 dozen doughnuts

Twenty-Five

Ya Habibi, Ya Ahlbi

If my mother happened to say, "Mama, bring me a glass of water," I understood that she was asking *me* for water, not her mother. I would have understood this even if we weren't the only two people in the room and my grandmother wasn't six thousand miles away in Damascus. Mama called my brother "Mama," too, and my sister. It was something Arab parents did, addressing their child by the appellation of their relationship to that child; as in my father's "Go on, Baba, wash your hands before dinner." All our relatives did that, as well. I grew up being called "Uncle" by my uncles, "Auntie" by my aunts—most of whom, to further confuse matters, weren't really aunts or uncles but were respected as such by the fact of simply being elder members of our community. You'd think this practice might confuse the kids, and yet none of us were, not ever, maybe because we recognized an endearment when we heard one.

Arabic, infamous for its curses, also abounds in so many endearments that as a child I was very rarely addressed by my given name. Instead, I was: *habibi* (my beloved), *ahlbi* (my heart), *adami* (my bones), *rohi* (my life breath), *deeni* (my faith), *senadi* (my support). And one of the strangest, yet to me most endearing of all, *ti'bourni* (may you bury me).

Of course, we had our formal given names, too. The Syro-Lebanese Catholic culture of the mid-twentieth century, like the Russian of the previous century, admired all things French, and we'd all been given French counterparts to our Arabic names: my sister was baptized Geneviève, my brother Albert (no final *t* sound!), and my name was pronounced as if the *s* were a *z*, as in "Joz-AYFF." In Arabic I was Yousef, but I hardly ever heard myself called that either. Among family I was usually just Zuzu, the Arabic diminutive for Yousef. A baby name. So, shortly after I started first grade, I began insisting that my parents call me Joe. Which they did, eventually. Around my senior year in high school.

A son didn't name himself, not in the Arab culture I was born into. There was a tradition to naming, a convoluted protocol that went something like this: the firstborn son names his own firstborn son after his father (the child's grandfather), and that son in turn names his firstborn son after *his* father. Example: Braheem the son of Khalil names his firstborn son Khalil after his father; years later this same Khalil (the son of Braheem) will name his own firstborn son Braheem. And on it goes, the same two names never dying out but leapfrogging from past to future, past to future. Second-born sons, like me, were usually named after uncles or grand uncles.

There's more. The firstborn son doesn't exactly keep his given name … nor does his father keep *his* own given name.

Example: While Khalil is a child, he will be called Ibn Braheem (the son of Braheem). And after Khalil is grown up and names his own firstborn Braheem, he (Khalil) will forever after be known not as Khalil but as Abou Braheem, the father of Braheem. So, in a way, the son of his father becomes the father of his father.

You'd think there would be an identity crisis in here somewhere. But oddly enough, there isn't. In our culture you are known by your relationships to others, those people to whom you are inextricably tied. You just knew who was who. Just as when my mother said, "Mama, bring me water," I knew she was addressing only me.

When I was in third grade, my brother and I urged Mama to sign us up for the new Cub Scout troop that was forming at school. Uniforms, saluting the flag—it sounded like the American thing to do, so, yes, she agreed. But when the den mother, taking information, asked for our middle names, Mama hesitated, seemed perplexed. She looked at my brother and me as if we held the answer. But we didn't. My brother and I looked back, waiting for her answer. We knew *ya ahlbi* and *ya senadi* and *ya habibi* and all those other endearments, but middle names? We didn't know we even *had* middle names. Which we didn't. Until Mama pointed to my brother, Albert, and said his middle name was Joseph. Then she pointed to me and said that my middle name was Albert. Then, she gave an abrupt little nod. That settled it. From here on I was Joseph Albert. Later, when we questioned her about why we'd never before known our middle names, she gave a dismissive flip of the wrist. "*Yallah!*"

➹ ➹ ➹

When I was in eighth grade, Sister Esther gave a lesson about names and why Catholic parents often give their children saints' names. She explained that names were more than identifying tags, that in fact they actually *meant* something. Sister opened a little pamphlet that listed Christian names and their meanings. Of course, everybody in class wanted to know what their own names meant. Since Sister Esther—like all the nuns—was partial to the girls, they went first. Barbara, we learned means "foreign." Shirley was "bright clearing," Margaret was "pearl." And so on. When Sister finally turned to the boys, I learned that Joseph came from the Hebrew for "increase." Cool, I remember thinking. Then someone wondered aloud whether our last names had meanings too. Of course, Sister said. Some, like Johnson (John's son) and Taylor (tailor) were easy to figure out, but for the others she suggested we ask our parents.

I went to my mother first. Looking up from her work—she was threading fresh okra into necklaces for hanging to dry—she replied with a wry smile that her maiden name, Akel, meant "wise" or "enlightened." As for Geha (in Arabic pronounced *Jeha*), well . . . her smile turned hesitant . . . well, my father could tell me about that one. She seemed to be skirting the issue, and that put me on guard. As if I wasn't already tentative enough about asking my father. Not that he wouldn't have an answer; I was sure he would. But like his conviction that the Lebanese discovered America and invented chess and the ice cream cone, it was hard telling what his answer might be.

And, sure enough, he didn't disappoint.

"Yes, Baba, it means something," he said, leaning toward me across the table. "*Jeha*, it's a big name."

Big? Uh oh. "Big, how?"

"Big famous!"

"You mean there's lots of people with our name?"

"I mean *famous*!"

"Okay, okay. But does the name itself *mean* anything? In Arabic?"

"Yeah, shore it does. It mean"—he paused a moment, thinking how exactly to put this—"de clown."

"The clown?"

"Yeah."

"As in a *circus* clown?"

"Yep, sorta like dat. The funny guy. Whatchamacallit," he touched a finger to his temple. "The funny guy for the king."

"The fool?"

"That's it. The guy he's simple."

"Simpleton? Fool?"

"You betcha!"

I groaned. Why did I even ask?

➤➤➤

In the summer, my mother used to dry fresh okra by spreading the pods on a cloth in the sun; next day, she'd take needle and thread and fashion "necklaces" of the pods, which she'd hang on the back porch to continue drying. Thus, we were able to enjoy hearty okra stews throughout the winter. Nowadays, I just look in the frozen vegetables department.

Mom's Baymee bi Djaaj
(Okra-Chicken Stew)

1½ tablespoons olive oil
1½ tablespoons butter
2 pounds (or so) chicken pieces: 2 wings, 2 legs, 2 thighs
1 medium onion, diced
2 garlic cloves, minced
1 teaspoon salt
½ teaspoon black pepper
1½ tablespoons ground coriander
1 can (14.5 ounces) whole tomatoes
2 tablespoons tomato paste
Pinch of sugar
2½ cups chicken broth
2 pounds fresh okra, rinsed, tops of stems cut off
2 lemons, juiced, divided
¼ cup chopped fresh cilantro

1. Heat olive oil and butter in a Dutch oven and sauté chicken till lightly browned. Remove chicken from pan and reserve.
2. Fry onion in the oil till translucent, then stir in the garlic, salt, pepper, and coriander. Stir 1 minute.
3. Add the tomatoes, tomato paste, sugar, and broth. Bring to just boiling, then lower heat to a simmer.

4. Stir in the okra, along with the juice of 1 lemon. Top with chicken pieces and cover. Let simmer 30 to 40 minutes.
5. Remove from heat. Before plating, stir in the remaining lemon juice. Sprinkle with cilantro and serve with rice, garnished with lemon slices and sprigs of cilantro.

TIPS:
- Some cooks suggest reducing okra's natural "gummy" quality by browning it under the broiler before adding to the stew. Others like the gumminess just fine, considering it the signature texture of an okra dish.
- Baymee bi Djaaj can easily be made vegetarian, or *siami*, by substituting chickpeas for the meat and vegetable broth for the chicken broth.

Twenty-Six

Jeha the Simple

"But Jeha," Baba continued, "he's the kinda fool he's also smart, too. Y'know?"

Yeah, I knew. I knew that according to my father my full name now meant . . . increase clown.

"Every place inna world where people talkin' Arabic," Baba continued, "they tell the *Jeha* stories." He raised one hand and used it to describe an encompassing arc, "You hear Jeha stories all roun' the world."

"Then how come I never heard any Jeha stories?"

"Cause you don' listen."

"I'm listening now."

➤ ➤ ➤

One morning Jeha the Simple knocked on his neighbor's door and asked to borrow a certain stewpot. The neighbor agreed, but only reluctantly. The pot was expensive after all, sheathed in burnished copper. Jeha promised, hand to heaven, that he would return it in three days' time.

Three days passed, and again there came a knock at the neighbor's door. It was Jeha, and in his hands was the stewpot, freshly cleaned and polished. Heaving a sigh of relief, the neighbor took back the pot and immediately saw that inside it was nestled a small, but equally beautiful, copper pot.

"What's this?" he asked.

Jeha smiled. "While your pot was in my possession it gave birth."

"Gave birth?"

"Yes, and this is her baby."

"I see," the neighbor nodded solemnly. Then he smiled. The poor fellow wasn't called Jeha the Simple for nothing. "Of course," he said, accepting both pots.

A week passed. There came again a knock on the door, and once again there was Jeha asking to borrow the stewpot. "For three days only," he vowed.

"Only three?" The neighbor agreed at once, thinking to gain a sister to the little pot. "Keep it *six* days if you like!"

Well, three days passed, and no Jeha. Then six days. Three weeks passed, then six weeks. Finally, the neighbor came knocking on Jeha's door. "What's become of my brass stewpot?" he demanded.

"The pot?" Jeha burst into tears. "Oh, my dear neighbor, you haven't heard the news?"

"What news?"

"Your stewpot, poor thing . . . it has died."

"Died? Since when do stewpots *die?*"

Closing his door, Jeha replied, "Ever since they started giving birth!"

➔➔➔

There were more Jeha stories, and the more of them Dad told me, the more my skepticism increased. He had to be pulling them out of thin air, like the one about the king of Persia and the invention of chess (chess being *Jeha's* invention, of course!) or the one about Jeha and the donkey that shits gold lira. But it was several years after Dad had passed away, and I was off living on my own, teaching and writing, that my skepticism was stopped cold, as I came across an article in the *Saudi Aramco World* magazine. I was in the library researching background for a piece of fiction I'd set in the Middle East. What caught my eye was the graphic that accompanied the article. Beneath the title "A Man of Many Names" hung a cluster of similarly spelled names superimposed over one another: Jha, Nezzradin, Jofa, Goha . . . Geha! The writer was Paul Lunde, a linguist who according to the author's blurb had lived in Saudi Arabia and studied Arabic and Persian at the London School of Oriental Studies. The subject of his article was an Arab folk character, a "man of many names" and hundreds of stories, who happened to be, in Lunde's words, "a sort of inspired simpleton." In Egypt, this simpleton was named Goha, "in the Sudan, Jawha, in Algeria, Jeha, and in Morocco, Jha." In Lebanon and Syria he was Djeha or Geha. His stories, part of an established oral tradition, extended beyond the Arab world into Spain and southern France, to Malta and Sicily, up to northern Italy, "where he is called Jofa, Jufa, Jugale, Jugane, Giuvale, and Giucca," then around the Adriatic and into the Balkans, Greece, Turkey, and out to the steppes of Russia.

Apparently, the stories were as well known as Dad had claimed all those years ago. What's more, there was even a book written, *Goha the Simple*, published in 1919. Lunde says it came close to winning the prestigious Prix Goncourt (the prize that year was awarded instead to Marcel Proust). The book was translated into seven languages, later was turned into a play, and in 1958 it was made into a movie, *Goha*, starring Omar Sharif and Claudia Cardinale, and it won the Jury Prize that year at the Cannes Film Festival.

All totally surprising to me, of course, but Lunde's conclusion was the most surprising of all: "It has been suggested that Cervantes got the idea, and perhaps even the title name, for his great work *Don Quixote* from Goha stories that were brought to Spain by the Moors. Cervantes spent some years as a prisoner in Algiers." Goha to Quixote? Maybe. After all, as Lunde pointed out, "what better way to while away the time in a dreary cell than by exchanging Goha stories with one's jailer?"

➔➔➔

Sopa de Ajo
(Spanish Garlic Soup)

In honor of Cervantes, here's one of my favorite Spanish recipes, a rustic soup created by shepherds who kept off the chill of those long cold nights outdoors by using up their day-old bread and leftover sausage bits. Add a little broth, a little paprika, and garlic, lots of garlic! Garlic is so essential, and not just to Mediterranean cuisine, that chefs around the world have called it the fifth element.

About 6 cups of day-old bread, crust removed, cubed
½ cup extra-virgin olive oil, divided
8 to 12 garlic cloves, thinly sliced
3 ounces ham, prosciutto, or Andouille sausage, diced
2 heaping teaspoons sweet paprika
6 cups chicken broth, plus more for thinner broth
¼ cup chopped Italian parsley, plus more whole sprigs for garnish
1 teaspoon salt
½ teaspoon black pepper
¼ teaspoon cayenne pepper (optional)
4 large eggs

1. Preheat oven to 350°F. Scatter bread cubes on a foil-lined sheet pan, drizzle with ¼ cup of the olive oil, and put in oven till they start to crisp, about 15 minutes.
2. Heat the remaining ¼ cup of olive oil in a Dutch oven on medium low. Add garlic and simmer till barely golden; add ham, stir, and raise heat to medium. Add paprika and stir; add crisped bread cubes and stir.
3. Add broth, raise heat to high, and bring to a boil. Turn heat down to medium; stir in parsley and add salt, black pepper, and cayenne. Add more broth if you prefer a thinner soup.
4. Make 4 separate indents in the soup with the back of the spoon, and carefully break an egg into each depression. Cover pot to poach. Cook until the whites are set and the yolks are beginning to firm but not yet hard, about 5 minutes. Garnish with parsley to serve.

Serves 4

➨ ➨ ➨

The following recipe isn't Lebanese in origin—it's not even Middle Eastern—but it is based on a West African dish that arrived in sub-Saharan Africa from the Mediterranean by way of Portuguese explorers. I first learned to make it from the firemen whose station was next door to my uncle's Red and White supermarket, where I worked summers and weekends in high school. The firemen were adventurous cooks and they were always over buying supplies for the different recipes they were trying out. On cold October evenings, as I pushed home the grocery carts for the babushka ladies, the aromas wafting out of the firehouse were damn near intoxicating.

Palaver Stew

2 pounds pork shoulder, cut into cubes
1½ tablespoons peanut oil
4 garlic cloves, thinly sliced
¼ cup sherry wine
1 can (12 ounces) ginger ale
1 teaspoon crushed red pepper flakes, or to taste
½ teaspoon black pepper
1 or 2 thumb-sized pieces ginger, cut into matchsticks
Several pieces candied ginger, cut into matchsticks
¼ cup brown sugar
1 medium onion, chopped
1 can (14.5 ounces) diced tomatoes

1 package (10 ounces) fresh spinach, divided
1 teaspoon salt, or to taste
Dash of cayenne pepper (optional)
1 sweet onion, halved and sliced into thin crescents
2 medium tomatoes, halved and sliced into thin crescents
¼ cup crunchy peanut butter
Dollop (or 2) honey

1. Using a large fry pan (with lid), brown pork in peanut oil. Transfer meat to a slow cooker set to medium high. Add garlic to fry pan, sauté 1 minute. Deglaze fry pan with sherry. Place contents of pan in the slow cooker with the meat.
2. Add ginger ale, red pepper flakes, black pepper, ginger, candied ginger, brown sugar, chopped onion, and the can of diced tomatoes to the slow cooker.
3. Cover and simmer 1½ hours.

Note: You can stop here, let cool, and refrigerate overnight. I recommend doing so since flavors improve in the fridge; also, if cooking for guests, the house won't smell of frying and the cook won't be too busy to visit.
To continue ...

4. Wash spinach and remove tough stems.
5. After slow cooker has simmered 1½ hours (or if finishing the next day, after stew is reheated), add a handful of spinach to wilt in stew. Add salt and cayenne pepper to taste.
6. Make couscous (see below). Place in large bowl or platter. (A large-rimmed pasta platter works well.)
7. Place remainder of spinach atop the hot couscous. Arrange sweet onion crescents atop the spinach and the tomato crescents atop the onions.
8. Stir peanut butter into the stew and cook 2 minutes or until slightly thickened. Stir in honey.
9. Pour hot stew onto arranged bed of couscous and serve immediately.

FOR THE COUSCOUS:

3 cups orange juice
2 cups couscous
½ teaspoon salt
2 tablespoons raisins, currants, or craisins
Zest of 1 orange
1 tablespoon toasted pine nuts

1. In a lidded saucepan, bring juice to a boil.
2. Stir in couscous, salt, and raisins; cover and remove from heat.
3. After 5 to 7 minutes, fluff couscous with a fork, top with orange zest and pine nuts and serve.

Serves 6 to 8

Twenty-Seven

Il Harim

When I was twenty-six, I traveled to the Middle East to finally lay eyes on the land where I was born and to reunite with relatives who hadn't seen me since I was a baby. In Damascus, my mother's hometown, an uncle walked me along the street called Straight, arguably the oldest continually used thoroughfare in the oldest continually inhabited city in the world. Visiting Lebanon, I spent a day in Zahlé, the mountain town where I was born, famed for its garden restaurants overlooking the Berdawni River. I stepped into the mud-brick hovel from which my father made his escape to America. Nearby, in the Bar Elias district, I visited the house—the very bedroom—in which I was born. And I was lucky enough to see Beirut in its heyday before the destruction of the civil war; back then, in 1971, Lebanon's cosmopolitan capital was known as the jewel of the Middle East, with its sidewalk cafés and fine restaurants ("the most gastronomically sophisticated city between Paris and Hong Kong," according to one guidebook), its casinos and beaches, and its jet-set clientele.

And yet, just as exciting to me was the other half of my journey, visiting relatives in Egypt. There, I strolled through Cairo's famed Khan el-Khalili Bazaar, where my Egyptian-Lebanese uncle was a jeweler in the gold souk; I took a train to Alexandria, the seaside city that Lawrence Durrell called "the winepress of love." Best of all, my cousin Raouf drove me to see the pyramids at Giza, just outside Cairo. In Egyptian Arabic the pyramids are called *il harim*, and I'll never forget my first glimpse of them. As Cousin Raouf drove, I eagerly scanned the sky above the rooftops, my newly bought 35-millimeter camera at the ready. We spoke little on that long drive out of Cairo. Raouf didn't know any English, and Egyptian Arabic was so different from Lebanese that it sounded to me like a different language entirely. My pathetic Kitchen Arabic was, of course, less than useless.

So it was mostly in silence that we wove our way through a shaded subdivision of tall apartment buildings that finally gave way to the open desertscape of the Giza plateau. But still, no sign of the pyramids. I was expecting something like what you'd experience driving west out of Nebraska and across the Colorado flatlands, how you finally sight the faraway little bumps on the horizon that would become the Rocky Mountains.

I struggled to put the Arabic words together in my mind before saying them aloud. "*Likun, feyn raiheen?*" (Hey, where are we going?)

Just then the car slowed out of a long wide curve, and Raouf held up one hand to indicate his side of the road. "*Il harim*," he said, as if introducing us. And suddenly there they were. The pyramids. I hadn't even seen them coming. They were blue in the distant haze, like an apparition. Still miles away, yet utterly enormous, their edges forming sun-glinted straight lines leading my eyes up, up, as I craned my neck to see the top of them through the windshield; it had to be some sort of optical illusion, they seemed so close. The effect was dreamlike, a majesty that the camera in my hands was useless to capture.

➤ ➤ ➤

We returned several times to Giza, and I could go on about how I beheld the face of the Great Sphinx, but "beheld" would be too fancy a word. Because for the entire two weeks I spent in Egypt, the Sphinx had a kite attached to its right ear, a white hexagonal paper kite whose string had somehow tangled itself in the stone. Sure, right there before me was the face that had gazed steadily and serenely upon the ages . . . upon Herodotus . . . Alexander the Great . . . Caesar . . . Napoleon . . . Muhammad Ali Pasha . . . Oh, I tried to summon the magnitude of it, I really did, but it was too much of an effort with that kite constantly flapping and wiggling side to side like an earring.

➤ ➤ ➤

Mloukhiyeh is a traditional dish of Egypt that some believe originated with the pharaohs (*mloukhiyeh* is Arabic for "food of the kings"); others claim it was first prepared by the ancient Jews of Alexandria (thus the plant's common English name, Jew's mallow). The dish was considered so tasty that in 1000 CE the Fatimid Caliph al-Hakim forbade it to all but the ruling class.

Made from a highly nutritious plant (*nalta* jute, or *Corchorus olitorius*) that nowadays can be found at Middle Eastern markets in frozen packets, like spinach, it takes on a mucilaginous texture when cooked, the way okra does. *Mloukhiyeh* is often prepared with rabbit, or in Alexandria with shrimp, and it's much prized for the viscous, gumbolike texture the mallow adds to soups and stews. Some Egyptian cooks "tame" this quality by adding chopped tomato for its acid; the Lebanese omit tomato and use vinegar-soaked onions instead. If you don't like the consistency of gumbo, this recipe works just fine with plain chopped spinach.

My mother served it to first timers with the warning that *mloukhiyeh*'s complicated flavors must grow on you: you probably won't like your first taste. (My wife, Fern, didn't.) But you'll enjoy it the second time you give it a try. (Fern did.) And after the third time, you will find yourself beginning to yearn for it. (Which she does!)

Here's my mom's recipe for Syrian-style *mloukhiyeh*.

Mloukhiyeh
(Egypt's Signature Dish)

2 tablespoons olive oil
1 medium onion, coarsely chopped
6 cups chicken stock
2 packages frozen *mloukhiyeh* (or 2 to 2½ cups dried)
1 store-bought rotisserie chicken, dark and white meat separated
1 small bunch cilantro, coarsely chopped, stems and all
6 garlic cloves, minced
2 tablespoons butter
2 teaspoons ground cumin
1 tablespoon ground coriander
1 teaspoon ground cinnamon
2 teaspoons allspice
1 teaspoon salt
1 teaspoon black pepper
Juice of 1 lemon

3 cups plain cooked rice (leftover from Chinese takeout works great,
    or make your own)
1 pound cooked kibbeh, crumbled (optional)
Pita bread, dried (and/or toasted) and broken up
2 medium onions, chopped, soaked overnight in mixture of 1 cup white
    vinegar and ½ cup water

1. Heat olive oil in a soup pot or Dutch oven, and sauté onion over medium
   heat until opaque (about 3 minutes).
2. Add chicken stock. Bring to a boil. Add *mloukhiyeh* and the dark meat
   from the rotisserie chicken. Bring to a boil again, add cilantro, reduce
   heat, and simmer for 15 to 20 minutes. Avoid undue stirring.
3. In a small fry pan, sauté garlic in butter over medium heat for about 2
   minutes; combine cumin, coriander, cinnamon, allspice, salt, and pepper,
   add to fry pan, and sauté 3 minutes. This spice combo is called the *ta'liya*.
   After sautéing, stir *ta'liya* into simmering soup.
4. Just before setting soup out to serve, add the lemon juice.

Meanwhile . . .

1. Place rice in a serving bowl.
2. Shred the chicken breast meat with forks or fingers; place in second
   serving bowl.
3. Heat the kibbeh (if using), and place in third serving bowl.
4. Set out the pita bread in a fourth serving bowl.
5. Place the vinegar-soaked onions in a glass or nonreactive serving bowl
   with a ladle.

TO SERVE:
Starting with broken pita in the bottom of the bowl, diners "build" their own
servings of *mloukhiyeh*, cafeteria-style, ladling soup, rice, crumbled kibbeh, a
little more soup, shredded chicken, maybe more soup, and topping it all off
with a ladleful of vinegar-soaked onions.

Serves 8

➔ ➔ ➔

Baharat is the Arabic word for "spices" and is often used as shorthand in Middle Eastern recipes for a mixture of seven (well, *usually* seven) spices. But which seven? Because the more I asked around the more I realized there are almost as many "authentic" Lebanese seven-spice mixes as there are Lebanese cooks. The most common spices among the "seven" include black pepper, allspice, coriander, cumin, clove, cinnamon, and nutmeg. Some might add cardamom to this mixture, or hot paprika, or ginger. Or fenugreek. (But not me.)

Here's my own recipe for a Lebanese seven-spice *baharat*, which is comprised of—in my case—*eight* spices:

Baharat
(Lebanese Spice Mix)

1 part black peppercorns
1 part cumin seeds
½ part coriander seeds
¼ part whole cloves
¾ part dried mint
1½ parts paprika
1 part ground cinnamon
¼ part ground nutmeg

1. Heat a small skillet over medium-high heat and dry roast the peppercorns, cumin seeds, coriander seeds, and whole cloves until they become fragrant, about 3 to 5 minutes, tossing regularly to prevent scorching.
2. Transfer them to a bowl and allow them to cool completely before grinding them in a spice grinder along with the mint, paprika, cinnamon, and nutmeg. Keep stored in glass jar.

TIP:
- Measured "to taste," Baharat can be used to add its signature flavor notes to a variety of dishes, ranging from meaty *kefta* to poultry to vegetarian *mjedderah*.

Twenty-Eight 🦎

More Room Outside . . .

On my first morning staying with relatives in the Gazirat Badran quarter of Old Cairo, I was awakened by the loud trumpet-pant of a donkey, HAW! HAW! I opened the shutters and stepped out onto the balcony to have a look. The street below was so narrow that automobiles were not permitted. Most people walked, a few rode bicycles or motor scooters. Causing something of a stir among the passersby was a man leading a donkey down the center of the street. The animal was heavily burdened by two enormous jars, one on either flank. The man holding its rope stopped every few yards and called out to the neighboring housewives, who soon swarmed the street holding out pans and pots of all sizes. The man deposited the coins they handed him in the folds of his *djellabiyeh*, which even from my vantage several stories up I could see was dingy and dirt flecked. Its arms, especially, looked smeared and stained reddish brown. I saw why when he wiped the ladle on his sleeve before dipping it into the jar and scooping the reddish-brown contents into the outstretched pans. I shook my head. *Wow*, I thought, *I'm sure glad I'm eating Aunt Odette's food while I'm here!*

The next day at breakfast, my aunt served us something she called *ful medames*, a most wonderful lemony-garlicky mashed-bean dish. "Auntie," I said, "this is so delicious, I gotta have your recipe!"

"No recipe, *habibi*," she replied. "I buy these from the man you looking at out the window yesterday."

"With the donkey?" I asked, weakly. She nodded, smiling.

Later that afternoon, I was violently sick and stayed that way for days on end. When I developed a fever, a doctor was summoned. Luckily, doctors still made house calls over there. He diagnosed "severe gastroenteritis" and prescribed medication. I remember in my fevered state trying to let him know, using my pathetic Kitchen Arabic, that it was "the beans, the beans, *il ful medames!*" that did this to me; and all the while he kept responding in heavily accented English, "I yundaztanz you. I zpeekz Ingeez! Over here you muz drink only bottle watah!"

After I recovered, everyone blamed my condition not on the beans but on the waters of the Nile. Indicating the kitchen spigot, my cousins chuckled as they quoted the old saying, "Who drinks from the Nile always returns ... again and again!"

They were probably right, there was enough lemon and garlic in those beans to kill anything. So I decided that it had to be the water and that I would drink only bottled water for the rest of my travels. Also, when I began feeling well enough to eat again, I began craving those beans. They were that good!

→ → →

Not only does Middle Eastern cuisine promote good health, but along with its antioxidants, its omega-rich fats, its fiber—especially its fiber—it can sometimes also promote an abundance of, well, gas. Falafel is notorious for this, as are fava bean dishes. Another is *mjedderah,* a delicious lentil-and-onion porridge. But the greatest culprit is arguably also the most popular of all Middle Eastern dishes: puréed chickpeas, also called *hummus bi tahini.* In Little Syria during the 1950s and the dawn of the atomic age, it was popularly called *nuclear* hummus.

When I was growing up, we sometimes had Amerkain over for dinner—maybe one of the parish priests, or a friend from school—and I remember feeling humiliated when, right there at the table, my father would burp. And I mean loudly, without the slightest attempt to suppress or disguise. The way Dad saw things, why shouldn't he? Burping showed appreciation for the food. And should the guest react with a chuckle or an embarrassed silence, Dad would simply smile at them and explain in English, "Mor' room-a outside than in-a-side!" On the other hand, he considered farting to be rude and insulting—outside the family, anyway. Inside the family, the release of intestinal gas was something akin to high comedy ... depending of course, like all comedy, on timing.

Just as the Inuit languages are supposed to contain many different names for the many different types of snow, I grew up with multiple Arabic words for intestinal gas. *Fuhs,* for example, is onomatopoetic, sounding like what it represents: the single, brief breaking of wind. But for the occurrence of multiple *fuhses,* delivered one right after the other in a rat-a-tat-tat fashion, for that Arabic has another word, *d'rrata*, which again employs onomatopoeia. When the *d'rrata* surprises you, escapes from you unbidden and without warning, that's called *d'rrata filtani*. A runaway. And for the silent stinker, there is the almost whisper of a name—*fuhsweh*.

Darrit is the verb form. Which recalls to me these lines from an Arabic nursery rhyme my mother used to recite to us:

> *Mara ou yijal a'deen bil finjan*
> *Darratit il mara, tarr il yijal!*

> (A lady and a gentleman sitting inside a teacup,
> The lady farted, the gentleman flew up!)

A bit of nonsense about as meaningful as "Little Jack Horner" or the dish running away with the spoon. When I was a child, though, I thought it was pretty funny. I still do.

➜ ➜ ➜

Ful Medames
(Egyptian Breakfast Beans)

1 can (14 ounces) small fava beans
4 tablespoons extra-virgin olive oil, divided, plus extra for serving
1 medium onion, diced small
½ teaspoon salt
3 garlic cloves, minced, divided
1 teaspoon smoked paprika
¼ teaspoon cayenne pepper
½ teaspoon ground cumin
Juice of 2 lemons, or about 5 to 6 tablespoons, plus extra for serving
¼ cup chopped parsley

1. Rinse and drain beans. Using a fork or ricer, lightly mash about ½ to ⅔ of the beans.
2. Heat 2 tablespoons of the olive oil in a medium-to-large fry pan over medium-high heat. Sprinkle onion with salt and fry till translucent, then lower heat to medium low and add garlic. Sauté another minute or 2.
3. Stir in paprika, cayenne, and cumin. Wait about 30 seconds, then stir in the beans. Stir in the remaining 2 tablespoons of the olive oil.
4. Continue to cook over medium low for another 5 or 6 minutes. Stir in the lemon juice and remove from heat.

5. Plate mounded on a dish. Add a drizzle more of olive oil and lemon juice. Sprinkle with chopped parsley. Garnish with lemon wedges, quartered hard-boiled eggs, and/or sweet onion wedges. (The sweet onion wedges are easy to make and a great accompaniment: Cut 1 or 2 small onions into quarters and put in a jar with water to cover. Drizzle in a few drops of vinegar and let sit overnight in the fridge.)

➺➺➺

There is a sensitivity to fava beans, called favism, that is experienced by a small number of people—most of them of African or Mediterranean origin. It's rare, but people can die from it. That's the bad news. The good news is that people with favism seem also to be to varying degrees immune to malaria.

I learned this from Tim, one of the doctors in my poker group. Some years back Tim came to a cooking demo where I was making *ful bi laham*, and when I mentioned that some people might have a sensitivity to fava beans, called favism, he recited from memory its medical name, glucose-6-phosphate dehydrogenase deficiency. I was amazed, but he just shrugged, "The things you remember twenty years out of medical school."

Below is a recipe for the kind of *ful*, or fava bean, that I grew up eating; known as the broad bean or horse bean, it's much larger than the Egyptian *ful medames*.

Ful bi Laham
(Fava Beans with Lamb Shanks)

THE SHANKS:
2 lamb shanks (ask butcher to saw them in half crosswise; this will help release the marrow)
1 tablespoon ground cinnamon
½ tablespoon ground allspice
½ teaspoon salt
½ teaspoon black pepper
½ onion, sliced in slivers
1 garlic clove, thinly sliced
4 teaspoons olive oil, divided

1. Preheat oven to 400°F.
2. Rub shanks in cinnamon, allspice, salt, and pepper.
3. Place both halves of a lamb shank on each of 2 sheets of aluminum foil.
4. Divide onions and garlic, place on top of shanks, drizzle each shank with about 1 teaspoon of the olive oil, and wrap each tightly in foil.

5. Take more foil to double wrap each shank. Place on a cookie sheet and put in oven.
6. Immediately turn heat down to 250°F. Cook for about 5 hours.

THE FAVA BEANS:
1 tablespoon olive oil
1 tablespoon butter
1 medium onion, cut in slivers
1 tablespoon ground cinnamon
½ tablespoon ground allspice
1 tablespoon brown sugar
1 bunch cilantro, chopped
1 teaspoon salt
1 teaspoon black pepper
1 tablespoon ground coriander
2 garlic cloves, minced, or more to taste
½ red bell pepper, sliced in strips
1 can (19 ounces) large fava beans, drained and rinsed
    (I use Progresso brand)
1 cup beef stock, or more for thinning
¼ cup lemon juice
2 tablespoons cilantro, chopped fine
Lemon slices, to garnish

1. Add the oil and butter to a Dutch oven and sauté onions over medium heat until limp and transparent. Stir in cinnamon, allspice, and brown sugar. Add cilantro, salt, and pepper. Stir in coriander, garlic, and the red bell pepper.
2. Stir in fava beans. Add beef stock. Set to medium heat, cover, and let simmer 10 to 15 minutes.
3. Remove the shanks from the oven, carefully unwrap, and using a tong, lift them out of their grease and place them, bones and all, in the pan with the beans. Let simmer another 10 minutes. Add lemon juice right after you turn off the fire. Sprinkle on the cilantro.
4. Serve over rice, piping hot, with a dollop of ice-cold sour cream or *labneh* (Greek yogurt) on top. Garnish each serving with a lemon slice.

→→→

Of all the Middle Eastern street foods, one of the most popular has to be falafel, or as it's known in Egypt, *tamiyeh*. What makes this recipe Egyptian is the fava beans.

Tamiyeh
(Egyptian-Style Falafel)

TAHINI SAUCE:
3 tablespoons tahini paste
3 tablespoons lemon juice
3 tablespoons water, plus more if necessary
1 garlic clove, minced and mashed
¼ teaspoon salt
¼ teaspoon black pepper
Pinch of cayenne pepper

Combine the ingredients and whisk to a smooth consistency.

LABAN SAUCE:
1½ tablespoons lemon juice
1 tablespoon dried mint
1 garlic clove, minced and mashed
1½ tablespoons olive oil
1 teaspoon salt
8 ounces plain yogurt

Whisk the first 5 ingredients into the yogurt; keep ice cold till ready to serve.

SALAD:
2 cups chopped romaine lettuce
4 medium tomatoes, diced
1 medium cucumber, peeled, seeded, and chopped
1 large sweet onion, chopped and soaked overnight in water to cover and 1
    teaspoon vinegar
6 to 8 pita pocket bread loaves, sliced in half

FALAFEL:
1 can (15 ounces) chickpeas, drained and rinsed
1 can (15 ounces) small fava beans, drained and rinsed
½ cup minced onion
4 garlic cloves, minced
3 teaspoons ground cumin

¼ teaspoon cayenne pepper
1 teaspoon ground coriander
1 teaspoon salt
1 teaspoon baking soda
1 tablespoon lemon juice
½ cup cilantro leaves
½ cup parsley leaves
3 tablespoons olive oil, divided
½ cup toasted sesame seeds, or ½ cup panko (optional)
Olive oil cooking spray (such as Pam)

1. Preheat oven to 425°F.
2. In the bowl of a food processor, combine chickpeas, fava beans, minced onion, garlic, cumin, cayenne, coriander, salt, baking soda, lemon juice, cilantro, parsley, and 2 tablespoons of the olive oil. Pulse for 10 seconds. Stop and scrape down sides of bowl, then pulse for another 10 seconds, until all ingredients are well incorporated but mixture is still slightly coarse and grainy.
3. Form mixture into 25 to 30 ping-pong-size balls (optional: then roll in sesame seeds or panko). Let rest in fridge for 1 to 2 hours, or overnight.
4. Place falafel balls on a cookie sheet that has been brushed with the remaining 1 tablespoon of olive oil. Spray falafel well with olive oil cooking spray and bake for 15 minutes. Flip falafel, respray, and bake an additional 10 minutes, until falafel balls are crisp and browned.
5. Meanwhile, prepare sauces, toss together salad lettuce, tomatoes, and cucumbers in a bowl. Warm pita bread for 2 minutes in oven.
6. Fill each half-pita with ½ cup salad, 2 to 3 falafel balls, a sprinkle of the chopped vinegary onions, and 2 to 3 tablespoons of either sauce (or both, mixed).

Serves 8 to 12

Twenty-Nine

The Proustian Effect

The farther the people of my growing up recede from me in time and distance, the closer I come to see the foods of our heritage as providing more than just nourishment; the aromas and flavors of our cooking are also pathways to memory. For me, all it takes sometimes is the slightest taste, or a whiff of something on the stove, and in an immediate, even emotional way, I recall my childhood, feel once again the near-physical presence of my parents, my aunts and cousins, all long gone now.

There's a scientific reason that the sense of smell, and to some extent taste, can trigger strong memories and deep, intensely felt emotions. The human brain's olfactory bulb that registers smell (and to some extent taste) is "wired" close by the almond-shaped amygdala, where emotion is processed, and to the hippocampus, where memories form. Psychologists call the phenomenon of memory triggered by smell the Proustian effect after Marcel Proust, the French novelist who famously had such an experience while tasting a cookie dipped in blossom tea that his aunt used to make for him as a child. Proust used this moment as the impetus for the flood of memories that informed his multivolume novel, *Remembrance of Things Past*.

➜ ➜ ➜

Lucky are those of us who have had loving associations to go with those aromas and flavors, and the recipes with which to summon them. Some memories, however, I don't want to stir up—like fenugreek. There are people who love the taste of this spice, but I'm not one of them. Common sense tells us that all spices should be used cautiously because using too much or too little can truly make or ruin a dish; or, as Paracelsus the Renaissance medical pioneer put it, no poison but in the dose.

Except for fenugreek. For me, it seems, even a little is too much. Although it is commonly found in Middle Eastern and South Asian cuisines, fenugreek wasn't a spice I grew up with. In fact, I first—and last—tasted it in Egypt, as the primary flavoring for *basturma*, a dried beef, lunchmeatlike product. My brother, who loves the stuff, urged me to try it. Its pungent flavor was like nothing I'd experienced before. My lips and tongue felt numbed as if I wasn't eating food at all but something chemical or medicinal. And the long-lasting aftertaste! I would later research the spice and learn just what strong stuff it is: not only can fenugreek interfere with certain medications, especially antidiabetics and anticoagulants, it also can trigger allergic reactions in people sensitive to peanuts and chickpeas. The seeds have been known to prevent gas, but also to cause it … along with causing strong-smelling perspiration, and often lending a maple syrup–like smell to urine or to breast milk.

And yet many people—my brother for one—love the flavor for exactly the sharp piquancy that I so dislike. The ancient Romans had a saying: *De gustibus non est disputandum* (There's no disputing taste). With that in mind, I checked and found that *basturma* is available online. So, who knows, you might want to give it a try yourself!

➤ ➤ ➤

Some tastes, it's believed, don't come naturally but are acquired, you must learn to long for them. For one person it might be *mloukhiyeh*, for another the fire-crisped edge of fat on a morsel of *laham mishweh*. For Richard the Uber driver, it was *toum*.

During a recent visit to Atlanta, my Uber driver, Richard, and I got chatting, and when he learned that I was a retired English teacher, he informed me that some years ago he had taught English himself, far away in Lebanon. He marveled at the coincidence when I told him that I was Lebanese, and immediately he switched to fluent Arabic. I was taken aback. From the look of this guy, I'd sooner expect Swedish or Norwegian! I understood that he was making small talk, and I tried to reply in kind. But, embarrassed at having to resort to my clumsy Kitchen Arabic, I soon gave up and explained that I just didn't have the vocabulary anymore. Switching back to English, Richard told me that he understood and went on about how much he'd loved the food in Lebanon. The flavors, the textures! And what taste did he miss the most? he asked rhetorically. "*Toum!*"

Toum? Yet another coincidence! There's a kitchen supply store near my home, I explained, called Cooks' Emporium, where I've been doing cooking demonstrations for the last twenty-five years. "Richard, I gave a demo of making *toum* just last weekend!"

"And did they love it?"

"Of course they loved it, just like everybody else I know who ever tasted *toum*!"

Not a dish in and of itself, *toum* is a fluffy white emulsion, more like a cross between a sauce and a condiment. In Middle Eastern cuisine it is used primarily as an accompanying flavor, much like mayonnaise or aioli, and provides a lemony-garlicky finish to a number of dishes.

When I explained that I had recently added *toum* to a book I was currently writing based on family recipes I grew up with, Richard asked if my version of *toum* was a family recipe.

I shook my head no. Neither my father nor my mother ever made it. Back then, nobody had the time, much less the energy, to sit half the day with a mortar and pestle, mashing, stirring, drizzling, whisking. No wonder so few, even in the Old Country, have ever tasted it outside a restaurant—and Lebanese restaurants are often judged by the quality of their *toum*. But all that was before the days of immersion blenders and the internet.

The toum recipe I learned to make was passed on to me from a friend of a friend who first saw it shared on the internet. That's the best I can do for a pedigree, but the recipe not only works, just as important is the technique, and that works too. Because most modern recipes involve using a food processor, the *toum* they create often ends up "breaking" like a failed sauce. But not with this technique, which is foolproof, as long as you make sure that at the start all ingredients and equipment are perfectly dry and at room temperature, and that the processing is done with an immersion or "stick" blender. So, from the far reaches of the internet, here's my version of the modern, foolproof *toum* recipe, especially for Richard the Uber driver, whose command of Arabic put me to shame.

Toum
(Garlic Purée)

6 to 8 garlic cloves, peeled
1 teaspoon salt
Pinch of citric acid (optional)
1 egg white
1 tablespoon water
1 tablespoon lemon juice
1 cup canola oil

Important Note: Be sure equipment is perfectly dry and all ingredients are at room temperature.

1. Place garlic, salt, and citric acid (if using) in the canister of a stick blender (or wide-mouthed mason jar). Blend till garlic is pretty well mashed up.
2. Add egg white, water, lemon juice, and oil to canister. Allow ingredients to settle (about 20 to 30 seconds).
3. Blend, beginning with the stick blender pressed to the very bottom; when ingredients appear to be emulsifying about halfway up the canister, gradually raise the blender by small increments until all contents are emulsified.
4. Serve immediately or store in a tight-sealed jar in the fridge for up to a month.

➤➤➤

Toum is great for making garlic bread or any sort of roasted meat but is at its best slathered on either *shish tawooq mishweh* (chicken kebabs) or on *kefta*, the *lamburger* of my youth. Just as growing up American had meant being called Joe and not Zuzu, so too did eating American food. And what food is more American than a hamburger? For me, personally, the word itself signified America. Maybe because, learning English, we had such trouble saying the word *hamburger*. I don't remember how we mispronounced it, only that neighborhood kids teased us for our accent whenever we tried saying it. We did learn, finally, but getting the hang of that one word was, to me, almost an American achievement.

Because I so urgently felt the need to be American through and through, I pleaded with Mama to make us hamburgers. Being a good sport, she not only agreed, she decided to do the *Amerkain* one better by using ground lamb and mixing cilantro and onions and some of her own spices into it. Her American lamburger turned out to be *kefta*, disguised by flattening it into a patty and topping it with a bun.

The traditional version of *kefta* is an entirely different matter. No buns, and instead of ketchup or a slice of cheese, you'll want *toum*, and plenty of it!

Kefta
(Mama's Lamburger)

1 onion, chopped into large pieces
½ cup chopped parsley
½ cup chopped fresh cilantro
½ cup chopped fresh mint
4 garlic cloves, crushed
1 teaspoon ground cumin
1 tablespoon ground cinnamon
1 tablespoon paprika
Pinch of nutmeg
Pinch of red pepper flakes
1 teaspoon salt
½ teaspoon black pepper
1½ pounds ground lamb (not too lean!)
1 or 2 tablespoons olive oil

1. Place first 12 ingredients in a food processor and process, pausing to scrape down the sides with a spatula, until smooth.
2. Add the lamb and process all together. Transfer to large bowl and hand knead mixture, adding a few drops of olive oil for moisture.
3. Forming a handful about the size and shape of an egg, press this onto a skewer and roll on a flat surface until the egg is the shape of a fat cigar.
4. Place the finished skewers in the fridge for at least 1 hour before cooking.
5. Cook skewers on a grill or fry in a pan over medium-high heat, turning with a spatula or tongs to cook evenly (4 to 5 minutes per side).
6. Serve with pita bread and *toum*.

➝➝➝

The following recipe for Shish Tawooq Mishweh is for an appetizer dish, although it is traditionally served as an entrée. In which case, the recipe remains the same, just use bigger skewers!

Shish Tawooq Mishweh
(Chicken Kebabs)

THE MARINADE:
¼ cup plain yogurt
1 tablespoon onion powder
1 teaspoon salt
¼ cup tomato paste
½ teaspoon black pepper
½ teaspoon allspice
1 teaspoon ground cinnamon
½ teaspoon Aleppo pepper (optional)

THE KEBABS:
1½ pounds boneless, skinless chicken breast, cut into ¾-inch cubes
1 small sweet onion, quartered
1 red bell pepper, cut into ¾-inch squares
1 green bell pepper, cut into ¾-inch squares
2 dozen bamboo toothpicks
½ cup pomegranate molasses

1. Mix together all marinade ingredients, then add the chicken. Marinate in the fridge for at least 2 hours or as long as overnight.
2. Separate onion quarters into leaves, and soak in water in the fridge at least 2 hours or as long as overnight.
3. Soak bamboo toothpicks in water for at least 2 hours or as long as overnight.
4. When ready to cook, wipe the marinade from the chicken and thread a piece of chicken onto a toothpick, then a slice of onion, another piece of chicken, and finish with a square of bell pepper for crunch, flavor, and visual appeal.
5. Preheat oven to broil. Cover a cookie sheet with aluminum foil and spray it with cooking spray; arrange the kebabs so they're not touching.
6. Brush kebabs with pomegranate molasses, and broil about 4 to 5 minutes. Turn, brush the other side, broil another 4 to 5 minutes.
7. Remove from broiler, tent with aluminum foil, and let rest 5 to 10 minutes before serving as appetizers with *toum* purée on the side.

Side Note: The word *mayonnaise*, by the way, has a Lebanese-Spanish connection. Carthage, the North African city-state that fought Rome for control of the western Mediterranean, was a Phoenician colony with strong ties to its mother city, Tyre. Who hasn't heard of Hannibal the Carthaginian? But less known is Hannibal's brother Mago, who helped his brother conquer much of the Iberian Peninsula. It was Mago (pronounced Mayo) who founded the Port of Mahón in the Balearics. And it was in the Port of Mahón that, centuries later, a cook stirred egg yolks into aioli and created the sauce we've come to know as mayonnaise!

Thirty

Wherever We Go, There We Are!

The phenomenon known as the Lebanese diaspora, which had its beginnings in Lebanon's political and economic upheavals of the 1860s and stretched on into the 1990s and the aftermath of the Lebanese Civil War, has resulted in more Lebanese living outside Lebanon's borders than within. Far more. By some estimates, fourteen million live outside its borders to about four million within. Embarking alone, in pairs, or sometimes in groups of multiple families, they traveled throughout Europe, Africa, Australia, and the Americas from Canada to Argentina. Like their Phoenician forebears, they created settlements wherever they traveled. As a happy result, all over the world we find ourselves bumping into one another. Or to borrow a popular saying, wherever we go, there we are!

No wonder my father had a habit—stemming from his on-the-road huckster days—of calling out in Arabic to any dark-haired, olive-complexioned stranger, *Are you one of us?* His doing that embarrassed me when I was a kid. Looking back now, though, I'm amazed at how often his question—uttered in a city of strangers, all babbling a strange language—had in fact received back a sudden smile and an *Ahlan wa sahlan aleik.* For Baba it was like the sun coming out.

My father loved telling his story about encountering his own sister on the ship's ramp back in 1929 and somehow recognizing her. Half-siblings who'd never laid eyes on one another before, can you believe it? "Small world," his listeners would nod their heads and agree. What else can be said in the face of such an astounding coincidence? You have to be careful about coincidence because it can sometimes seem more kismet than happenstance. So you say something neutral, like "small world."

And then, of course, you offer a coincidence or two of your own.

For example, the time just a few years ago, when I was volunteering on medical missions as a surgical assistant (read dishwasher) to some of my MD poker buddies. On the last night of one of our trips to the Dominican Republic, we were driven from the mission hospital on the outskirts of La Romana (population 120,000) deep into the city to a restaurant where we sat at benches and were served, to my utter surprise, a Lebanese *maza* starting with kibbeh, pickled turnips, *t'lamit za'atar*, and *phtire* (meat pies) with *laban*. Equally surprising were the Polaroid snapshots that covered the entire wall behind the cash register; all of them were of the owner posing with different customers, their names typed and taped beneath each photo. One of the names read "Elias Geha." The picture wasn't of my father, of course, but of a much younger fellow who happened to have the same name. Even so, La Romana, Dominican Republic, was the last place I expected to be eating kibbeh and seeing my father's name on a wall. Small world.

Speaking of my poker group, here's another coincidence arising from Lebanese mixing and mingling. Nearly twenty-five years ago, six friends and I began hosting a monthly poker game. One night, we were playing at the house of one of our longtime members, Ed Nassif. A pediatric allergist, Dr. Nassif had cared for my daughters when they were babies. Being Lebanese, he has that seemingly inborn sense of hospitality. His wife, Rania, is an excellent cook, and for poker nights when Ed hosts, she lays out not only the usual treats—baba ghanoush, hummus, sliced *jibneh* cheese with olives—but entire meals as well, everything from lemon chicken and *heshweh* to *t'lamit za'atar*. As you can imagine, whenever Ed hosts, we take quite a few snack breaks. It was during one of these breaks that the conversation turned to cruises. Someone mentioned river cruises in Europe, another preferred Caribbean cruises where you can snorkel or scuba dive. "Not for me," Ed said with a smile. "I've had it with rocking side to side on a boat. Three weeks on the *Vulcania* was enough!"

I couldn't believe my ears. "You came over on the *Vulcania*?"

Ed nodded. "My older brother and I, we came over together as kids."

"When?"

"1956."

"That was ten years after me!" I said. Here I was in Ames, Iowa, just about dead center in the United States of America, playing poker for the last twenty-or-so years with a guy who'd come over on the exact same boat I did.

Next morning, I emailed Ed a photo of the *Vulcania* that I'd found on the internet, along with a short history of the ship's years of service between Beirut, Marseilles, and New York. "Look familiar?" I asked.

Ed replied in his usual laconic style. "Small world," he wrote.

➤ ➤ ➤

I served spinach pies at poker only once, not just because they are somewhat time consuming to make but also because they disappeared so quickly. My Amerkain poker buddies like them that much. A different story from when I was a kid, and my mother packed the same spinach pies in my school lunch box. I remember how my schoolmates were weirded out by these little triangular pies filled with . . . "Ewww! Seaweed! He's eating seaweed!"

Of course it wasn't seaweed I was eating. I wouldn't eat seaweed till many, many years later, at a sushi restaurant. To me, *phtire sbinakh* is far less exotic but equally delicious.

Phtire Sbinakh
(Spinach Pies)

PHTIRE DOUGH:

1 package dry yeast
½ teaspoon sugar
1 to 1½ cups lukewarm water, divided
1½ teaspoons salt
3 cups all-purpose flour, plus more for dusting
¼ cup olive or canola oil

PHTIRE FILLING:

2 packages (10 ounces) frozen spinach, thawed, drained,
    then hand squeezed
1 large onion, finely chopped
⅓ cup olive oil
Juice of 4 lemons
1 teaspoon citric acid (rock lemon) (optional)
½ teaspoon allspice
1 teaspoon ground cinnamon
1 teaspoon salt
½ teaspoon black pepper
½ cup toasted pine nuts or walnut pieces
½ cup pomegranate arils (optional)

1. In a small bowl, dissolve the yeast and sugar in ¼ cup of the lukewarm water. Let sit to proof, about 5 to 10 minutes.
2. Using a large bowl, whisk salt into the flour. Add the oil and the dissolved yeast, and knead, gradually adding enough of the remaining lukewarm water (about 1 cup or so) to create a sticky dough.
3. Place dough onto a floured work space and knead until dough is tacky to the touch but leaves no residue on the hand.
4. Place dough in a lightly oiled bowl that's roomy enough to allow the dough to double in size. Cover with plastic wrap and let rest in a warm spot until dough has doubled in size (1 to 1½ hours).
5. Shape dough into balls about 1½ to 2 inches in diameter. Cover and let rise another 30 minutes.
6. Heat oven to 400°F.
7. In a large bowl, mix together ingredients for *phtire* filling in the order listed above.
8. Dust work counter with flour. Using fingertips, flatten the balls to rounds the thickness of pie dough and diameter of 3½ to 4 inches each.
9. Place 1 to 1½ tablespoons filling in the center of a round. (Be careful not to let any of the filling touch the outer rim of the round.) Using thumb and two fingers, raise three sides around the filling and toward the center, then pinch the three seams into a triangular pie.
10. Arrange pies on greased baking pan and bake till bottoms are lightly browned (about 10 minutes), then place under broiler to brown the tops (2 to 3 minutes).

Makes 18 to 20 pies

➤➤➤

We used to call the meat-filled version of the spinach pie recipe *phtire sfeeha*, although there appears to be some disagreement. Some sources claim that the open-faced meat version is properly called *sfeeha*, whereas *phtire* is the spinach-filled closed triangles (or cheese-and-onion-filled *phtire bi jibneh*). I think it probably depends on who you ask. As my niece, Lizzie, used to request them: "Ask Uncle Joe to send us more Geha's Sfeehas!"

Phtire Sfeeha
(Meat Pies)

MEAT FILLING:
2 pounds ground lamb
1 large onion, finely chopped
1 teaspoon salt
½ teaspoon black pepper
1 teaspoon allspice
2 teaspoons ground cinnamon
1 teaspoon citric acid (rock lemon)
¼ cup *labneh* (or Greek yogurt)
½ cup toasted pine nuts

Brown the lamb with onions and spices, then let cool. Mix *labneh* and pine nuts into the filling. All other preparation instructions are the same as for Phtire Sbinakh, including cooking time.

Note: Phtire sfeeha can be made as open-faced rounds. Follow to step 9 for Phtire Sbinakh, but after applying a tablespoon of filling, simply skip pinching them into triangles and go on to step 10.

Epilogue

We came to America to become Americans—and we exceeded!
—a saying that was popular among early generations
of Arab Americans, circa 1900 to 1925

"America will change you," my grandmother said to Mama upon our departure for America. "We will not see one another again." They embraced, and then she continued, adding that Old-Country adage of the left behind, "Don't forget who you are."

When Mama related this story to me, she made her mother's words sound regretful, less an admonishment than a sad statement of fact. America is big; a person can get lost there.

My own sense of lostness I trace back to that traumatic first day at Rosary Cathedral School; it was also the day that marked a major step forward in my becoming American. Because of school, I would continue to abandon the language of my birth and say what I had to say—indeed to think my thoughts—in a different language. At home, of course, my family would continue to speak Arabic. But over the years, mingling with English, it would begin to sound less and less like Arabic. Everything changes.

Immigrants are usually complicit in the change that America imposes on them. "Making your own luck," the old-timers called it, which they did by finding work, any work, and laboring at it dawn to dusk, literally, so that their children wouldn't have to. Baba sent us to school in hopes we would surpass him, understanding how more and more with each new school year the memory of the Old Country would lose its grip on us, the old customs and values, its miseries and its special joys. And yet America gave us the chance to make our own luck. So, "God bless America," we said, always with full sincerity and not an ounce of irony.

My wife's grandfather, a Jew from Białystok who escaped the pogroms and poverty of Eastern Europe, used to sit in a lawn chair on the driveway of their suburban Long Island home, petting the family dog. "In America," he would marvel aloud to himself, "even a *dog* is lucky!"

And just as America changes us, we immigrants in turn change America. We contribute our loyalty to this country that took us in, we contribute the energy and the savvy and the will to succeed that brought us here. The art that helped form us now enriches the culture of America, along with the poetry and music and dance of our different heritages. Our religions diversify America, and so does the texture of our hair, the color of our skin. And because food, like a mother's touch, can evoke the very essence of home and caring and the loving handiwork of kin, we also contribute the cuisines of our heritage; we open bodegas, specialty groceries, ethnic restaurants, food trucks, and delicatessens and season the very taste of America.

➜ ➜ ➜

Back in 1993 I was still teaching, and as the end of fall semester approached, I had papers to mark—final exams, short story portfolios, master's theses. But I'd only recently learned to make *phtire sbinakh* according to Mama's recipe. I felt I was getting the hang of forming those little spinach-filled triangular pies, and I wanted to take a short break from grading to try out another batch or two. My wife, who had her own papers to finish, didn't object. She loved *phtire*. And besides, we had the whole weekend to finish up and get our grades in. In a way it felt as if the winter break had already begun. Sometime before school started again we were planning to visit family in Toledo. Usually, we'd wait for spring or summer break to make the drive, but my mother had been doing poorly lately, so we figured it was better to come sooner rather than later.

Monday morning arrived, and just as we got back from turning in our grades, we received a call from family in Toledo. My mother had taken a turn for the worse. As we hurriedly packed, I remembered to bag some of the *phtire* spinach pies for Mama to taste. They were her favorites, and I hoped a little taste might help brighten her spirits.

Next evening, as I walked into her hospital room, I was shocked by the look of her, so shrunken and gray. I realized I'd been lucky to arrive while she was still conscious. The nurses said she hadn't had any appetite for days. I sat at her bedside, and after we'd visited a while, she agreed to taste one of the *phtire* that I'd brought for her. Before taking a bite of the triangular pie, she paused briefly to look at it. I could see her considering its heft and proportions, evaluating what kind of job I'd done forming it. Then she took a bite. "Good," she said softly. But as she chewed, I could see she wasn't hungry, not in the least, and that she was having this taste for my sake alone. Always a good sport, my mother, even as she was dying.

I remember a pine nut had fallen and landed on the breast of her hospital gown. She looked down, picked it up and popped it in her mouth. The gesture was so her. Never one to waste food. When it was time to leave, I kissed her good night. As I opened the door, she called me back. "Next time," she said, indicating the *phtire* on her tray table, "more lemon."

That bite of *phtire* was the last food she ever ate. And those were the last words I heard her speak.

➤ ➤ ➤

A painting I completed recently depicts a family group expressing gratitude before eating, which I think is appropriate to a book about family and food. Titled *Grace: Iowa Picnic, 1936,* the picture is modeled after vintage photographs I'd come across that depicted Depression-era rural Iowans lifting their hats to say the blessing before a meal. As the painting was finishing up, I decided to add something personal. On the picnic table, in a corner of the picture, I'd painted a platter. It was empty. So now I piled it full with my mother's *phtire* spinach pies. That touch, like every recipe in this book, helps me remember who I am. Then I went ahead and added a wedge of lemon to the platter, too, just in case more lemon is needed.

Spices in Translation

ENGLISH	ARABIC
Anise	Yensoun
Basil	Habak
Bay Leaf	Warak Ghar
Black Pepper	Filful
Caraway	Karawehyeh
Cardamom	Hab il Hil
Cayenne Pepper	Filful Ahmar
Chili Powder	Filful Harr
Cinnamon	Kirfee
Clove	Kibsh Krinful
Coriander	Kizberrah
Cumin	Kamoun
Dill	Shabath
Fennel	Shamrah
Ginger	Zanjabeel
Marjoram	Mardakoosh
Mastic	Mistke
Nutmeg	Jawz il Tyeb
Parsley	Ba'dounis
Rosemary	Eklil al Jabel
Saffron	Za'faran
Sumac	Simak
Thyme	Za'atar
Turmeric	Karkem

Index to Recipes in English

Index to Recipes in Arabic

CRUX, THE GEORGIA SERIES IN LITERARY NONFICTION